LAS VEGAS

The Great American Playground

LAS VEGAS

The Great American Playground

EXPANDED EDITION

Robert D. McCracken

UNIVERSITY OF NEVADA PRESS
RENO, LAS VEGAS

UNIVERSITY OF NEVADA PRESS 89557 USA

Copyright ©1996 by Marion Street Publishing Company
New material copyright © 1997 by University of Nevada Press
University of Nevada Press edition published by arrangement with the author
All rights reserved
Manufactured in the United States of America

Designed by Debra Bradfield, Long Beach, California
Cover design by Erin Kirk New, Watkinsville, Georgia

Library of Congress Cataloging-in-Publication Data
      McCracken, Robert D.
      Las Vegas : the great American playground / Robert D. McCracken
      –Expanded ed.
      p.   cm.
      Includes bibliographical references and index.
      ISBN 0-87417-301-9 (alk. paper)
      1. Las Vegas (Nev.)–History. 2. Las Vegas (Nev.)–Description and travel. 3. Las Vegas
      (Nev.)–Economic conditions. 4. Business enterprises–Nevada–Las Vegas. I. Title.
F849.L35M39   1997
979.3´135–dc21   97-3272
                                         CIP

The paper used in this book meets the requirements of American National Standard
for Information Sciences — Permanence of Paper for Printed Library Materials,
ANSI Z39.48-1984. Binding materials were selected for strength and durability.

First Printing

06 05 04 03 02 01 00 99 98 97   5 4 3 2 1

*When astronauts aboard the space shuttle were in
orbit repairing the Hubble telescope in December 1993,
they looked down on the Earth at night.
"Las Vegas is outrageously bright,"
one astronaut remarked on return.
"You can see the Strip for 350 miles [up]."*

*This book is dedicated to those Las Vegas
pioneers who have lit up the night.*

Contents

PREFACE   ix
ACKNOWLEDGMENTS   xi

ONE   THE SETTING   1
     Location and Climate   1
     First Occupants   2
     The Southern Paiute   3

TWO   EARLY EXPLORATION   7
     The End of the Indian Way of Life   9
     The Mormon Mission of 1855   9

THREE   IN THE AFTERMATH OF THE GOLD DIGGERS:
     THE VALLEY IS SETTLED   13
     The First Ranches in Las Vegas   13
     Murder on the Kiel Ranch   16
     The Railroad Makes Plans for the Valley   18

FOUR   THE TOWN IS BORN   21
     The Rise and Fall of McWilliams's Townsite   21
     Clark's Townsite Auction   22
     Block 16: Where the Good Times Rolled   23
     The Town's First Hotels   27
     The Community Grows—Slowly   27
     The Strong-Minded People of North Las Vegas   28
     In the 1920s: Not a Roar but a Whimper   30

FIVE   DAMS, DICE, AND DIVORCE:
     LAS VEGAS IN THE 1930s   33
     The Building of Boulder Dam   33
     Sun City and the Model Community   37
     Earning Its Reputation   38

SIX   FEDERAL PROJECTS PROMOTE GROWTH   45
     The Birth of Nellis Air Force Base   45
     A Second Boom: Magnesium for the War Effort   46
     The Biggest "Boom" of All: The Nevada Test Site   48
     The Lombard Plane Crash   50

SEVEN   THE STRIP IS BORN—WITH THANKS TO
LOS ANGELES   53
     So Much for "Worthless" Property: El Rancho Vegas   53
     Second on the Scene: The (Last) Frontier   56
     The Flamingo Adds Some Color   60
     The Thunderbird   63
     The Golden Nugget Outshines the Rest   64
     The Campaign That Made the Desert Bloom   65

EIGHT   A DECADE OF DEVELOPMENT: THE 1950s   69
     The Desert Inn Sets the Pace   69
     In Quick Succession: The Sahara and the Sands   71
     Next on the Scene: The Showboat   75
     Standing Tall: The Riviera   76
     Upping the Ante: The Fremont   77
     Luxury First: The Tropicana   78
     Stardust: The Biggest of Them All   81
     A Convention Center Comes to Town   83

NINE   CORPORATE INVESTMENT: THE 1960s AND 1970s   87
     Howard Hughes Lands in Las Vegas   88
     Sarno's Magnificent Creations: Caesars Palace and
      Circus Circus   90
     Kirk Kerkorian Flies into Town   94
     Kerkorian's (MGM) Grand Dream   95
     Local Developers   97

TEN   A NEW IMAGE: THE 1980s AND BEYOND   99
     Modern History: Excalibur and Luxor   100
     Steve Wynn's Theme Resorts: The Mirage and
      Treasure Island   102
     Kerkorian Rises Again: MGM Grand Hotel,
      Casino, and Theme Park   104
     Stratosphere: Bob Stupak's Dream Tower   105
     Monte Carlo: Popular Elegance   107
     New York–New York: The Big Apple in Las Vegas   109
     Fremont Street Experience: Help for Downtown   110
     Bellagio: Steve Wynn Does It Again   112
     The Boom Continues   113
     Move Over, Broadway   115
     Neighborhood Casinos   117
     Roll 'Em: On Location in Las Vegas   118

ELEVEN   IN REMEMBRANCE   121
     The Dunes   121
     The Sands   124
     The Landmark   128
     The Hacienda

     EPILOGUE   131

     REFERENCES   133
     SUGGESTED READINGS   135
     MAP   136
     INDEX   141

Preface

Las Vegas is quite possibly the most unique city in the world; there truly is no other place like it. In Las Vegas, the city is the show.

Las Vegas! The name conjures a collection of images: To people around the world, it means fun, excitement, bright lights, entertainment, escape . . . or, more concretely, mega-sized hotels—the ten largest in the world—and casinos, measured in acres; luxurious showrooms; theme parks; monorails; marquees as large as office buildings, lit with the names of the biggest stars; shopping centers; specialty stores; and nearly every type of restaurant imaginable. The Las Vegas Strip has for decades far outshone the glitzy thoroughfare for which it was named—the Sunset Strip in Hollywood. One of the most interesting things about Las Vegas is how quickly it has grown from virtually nothing to its present size and stature as an international entertainment mecca. What is equally remarkable is that this development has taken place in the middle of an inhospitable desert. Ninety-five years ago, the valley in which Las Vegas now sits featured only a handful of small, dusty ranches, most of them only marginally profitable. By the late 1920s, Las Vegas had a population of only about 5,000.

The legalizing of easy divorce and gambling by the state of Nevada in 1931, combined with the construction of Hoover Dam about the same time, gave the small, isolated community the impetus it needed to grow. Further economic stimulus came with defense related activities in the Las Vegas Valley during World War II. After the war, Las Vegas visionaries took control of their own fate and began to actively promote the town as a fun and exciting place to visit. And did they succeed! Since then, no one has looked back—they have been too busy growing, planning, and making money.

In 1950, greater Las Vegas's population was under 50,000; by 1980, it had soared to 463,000. In 1990, the city's population stood at 753,000, and in 1995, it passed the million mark, with low estimates calling for a population of 1.5 million by the year 2007 and high estimates ranging up to 3 million. Numbers visiting Las Vegas have kept pace with the population boom. In 1970 (the first year for which figures are available), approximately 6.7 million people visited Las Vegas. By 1995, just twenty-five years later, the figure had swelled to nearly 30 million, with estimates of 40 to 50 million expected in just a few years. Las Vegas's airport has had to hustle to keep up with the torrid pace. In 1996, McCarran International Airport was the tenth-busiest airport in the nation in passenger volume, with 30 million passengers.

This book provides the reader with an overview and photographs illustrating Las Vegas's remarkable growth and success. The photos are among the very best available from the area's libraries, museums, and private sources. It is hoped that increased familiarity with Las Vegas's interesting history will help the reader better enjoy the area's many attractions and provide insight into how Las Vegas came to be The Great American Playground.

Robert D. McCracken

Acknowledgments

A special word of thanks is extended to the many people who assisted the author in preparing this volume.

The original manuscript was nearly 200 pages long, much too long for the type of book we had in mind. Rebecca Frazier helped in the difficult task of cutting it down to size and Michelle Starika Asakawa fine-tuned the editing, proofread the galleys, and provided production assistance. Michele Wynn and Bobette Host proofread final versions. Alice Levine assisted in additional editorial efforts. Their help is deeply appreciated.

Marion Swartz, Susan Kay, Stephanie Pas, and Jean Charney did the word processing, and Debra Bradfield did the design and layout. Erin Kirknew designed the cover. Susan Jarvis, along with Kathy War, University of Nevada, Las Vegas, Dickinson Library, Special Collections, provided research assistance and helped make photographs from the university's collection available. Nepwork Photos and the Las Vegas News Bureau were also extremely helpful in providing photos.

Donn Knepp, who knows more about Las Vegas entertainment history than anyone, Elizabeth von Till Warren, Susan Jarvis, and Jeanne Sharp Howerton critiqued the manuscript and photo captions. Kevin Rafferty, Community College of Southern Nevada critiqued the section on archaeology and W. Geoffrey Spaulding kindly provided instruction on wildlife living in the Las Vegas Valley 11,000 years ago.

A special thanks also goes to the late Roland Wiley, Clark County district attorney from 1939 through 1942, when construction on the Las Vegas Strip was just getting under way. Wiley answered numerous questions concerning the origins of the Strip as well as other aspects of Las Vegas history from 1929 (when he arrived) until his death in 1995.

Thanks to good friends Deke Lowe and Hank Records, southern Nevada old-timers now deceased, who answered many questions on Las Vegas history.

And another thank you to Margaret Dalrymple at the University of Nevada Press for creating the index to this expanded edition.

This book would not have been possible without the help of these people.

R.D.M.

LAS VEGAS

The Great American Playground

The Las Vegas Valley and a few of the plants and animals living in the area about 11,000 years ago. Hunters—Clovis people, the first known human occupants of the area—have just killed a horse with their spears, while a burro can be seen in the distance. See page 137 for further discussion of animals and plants pictured. Drawing by Gary Raham, Wellington, Colorado, with consulting by W. Geoffrey Spaulding

The Setting

Location and Climate

Las Vegas, Spanish for "the meadows," is located in the broad, arid Las Vegas Valley on the eastern edge of the Mojave Desert, about 30 miles west of the big bend of the Colorado River. The valley, approximately 40 miles long and 15 miles wide, ranges in elevation from 1,500 to 3,000 feet above sea level. It is rimmed on all sides by mountains, the highest of which is Charleston Peak (11,912 feet), which lies to the west and is one of the highest mountains between the Rocky Mountains and the Sierra Nevada.

Summers in the valley are hot and dry; temperatures can rise to more than 115° F., with very little measurable moisture. Winters are relatively mild, yet temperatures can fall to single-digit figures. Most of the valley's precipitation—on average about 4.6 inches a year—is received between December and March. Rain occasionally turns to snow, but the effect is nearly always short-lived.

Although Las Vegas is a desert city, old-timers can recall numerous springs that once existed throughout the valley, including large springs not far from downtown Las Vegas. In fact, Las Vegas took its name from meadows watered by a creek fed by the discharge of several springs located about 2 miles west of modern downtown Las Vegas. Most of the valley's springs dried up as a result of heavy pumping of groundwater that began in the early 1900s. Even so, the winter's rains give life to many flowering plants each April and May. Vegetation at other times of the year is scant over most of the valley; mesquite, salt grass, creosote, and rabbit brush are the main indigenous plants.

Las Vegas has the honor of being one of the most geographically isolated major cities in the continental United States. Los Angeles lies more than 270 miles—a 4-hour car ride—to the southwest. Salt Lake City lies 420 miles to the north; Phoenix is 290 miles to the south. Even farther away is Reno, Nevada, about 460 miles to the north. The nearest communities beyond the metropolitan complex, which are at least 40 miles away, include Indian Springs, Overton, and Pahrump.

Fancifully peering dimly 10,000 years into the past, Clovis hunters, one dressed as a bear, dance in the moonlight in the Las Vegas Valley. Painting by Don Wynn, Long Lake, New York

First Occupants

Bone and stone artifacts dating from about 11,000 years ago have been found at Tule Springs in the north end of the valley. The relics were probably left by members of the Clovis culture, nomadic hunters and gatherers who lived throughout North and South America at that time. Bones of mammoths, camels, horses, and giant sloths, all present then but which subsequently became extinct, have been found. The Clovis people are thought to have hunted these animals and collected many plants that grew along the streams and lakes then present in the canyons and valleys.

The next occupants of the Las Vegas Valley were the Lake Mojave people, who lived in the area between 10,000 and 7,500 years ago. They ranged over the desert of southern California and Nevada, hunting and gathering the seeds of wild plants that grew in the fairly lush areas bordering the many springs, streams, and lakes of the region.

Beginning about 9,000 years ago, the region became increasingly arid. As streams and lakes dried up, plant and animal life became correspondingly scarce. During this time the Lake Mojave culture is thought to have slowly transformed into what archaeologists call the Pinto Basin culture, which developed as a response to an ever more desiccated environment. These residents gradually moved to better-watered sites in the valley and occupied the region between 7,500 and 4,000 years ago.

The next period in the valley's archaeological history was marked by the Gypsum culture, which lasted until approximately 1,500 years ago and coincided with a time of greater precipitation in the area. The Gypsum culture is known for the unique stone tools and weapons its members produced, including leaf-shaped points and stone-flake scrapers as well as simple milling stones for grinding seeds. Petroglyphs found on the Mojave Desert from this period recorded the replacement of the atlatl (spear thrower) with the bow and arrow, which was more effective for hunting small game.

Beginning about 1,500 years ago, residents of the Las Vegas area experienced the intrusion of another culture into their territory. These newcomers, the Virgin Anasazi, were related in a distant way to the more complex Anasazi cultures centered in the Four Corners area.

The Virgin Anasazi residing in the Las Vegas Valley and the Muddy and Virgin River Valleys built small, single story pueblos contructed of adobe. They manufactured pottery and practiced agriculture (corn, beans, and squash) unlike the valley's earlier inhabitants. They established salt and turquoise mines in the region in order to participate in the larger trade networks operating out of the Four Corners area. For reasons that are not entirely clear, perhaps relating to drought or collapse of their trading network, the Anasazi abandoned the Las Vegas and Mojave Desert area in about the twelfth century. The Las Vegas area was then occupied exclusively by the ancestors of the modern Southern Paiute.

The Southern Paiute

The Southern Paiute Indians had resided in the Las Vegas Valley for hundreds of years when the first Europeans arrived in the 1820s. They are thought to have been organized into sixteen bands that ranged across southern Nevada, southeastern California, southwestern Utah, and northwestern Arizona. Each band was a relatively independent economic cluster that in turn was composed of several camps of families. Of the sixteen bands, the Las Vegas band occupied the largest geographical area. This band was known as the Nipakanticimi, meaning "people of Charleston Peak" (Kelly and Fowler, 1986:395). The Las Vegas band had camps at Las Vegas, Indian Springs, Ash Meadows, and Cottonwood Island on the Colorado River. Although they traveled on foot, the Southern Paiute could cover great distances, journeying even as far as the California coast to obtain shells for jewelry and "just to look around" (Kelly and Fowler, 1986:377).

The Southern Paiutes were primarily hunters and gatherers. Members of the band migrated throughout their vast territory, following the natural cycles of ripening plants, and usually maintained a base camp near a well-watered site. They gathered mesquite beans in the valleys and pine nuts in the Spring Mountains, as well as yucca and Joshua tree buds, agaves, and a variety of berries and grass seeds.

Rabbits, wood rats, chuckwallas (lizards), desert tortoises, and several species of birds were trapped or hunted along with an occasional bighorn sheep or deer. Small plots of irrigated crops, including corn and squash, were sometimes established near water sources. Stored foods were consumed during the winter; if cached stores ran out, juniper berries and Joshua tree shoots were eaten.

The Southern Paiute made a variety of baskets for food storage, transportation, and preparation; baskets covered with pitch were used as water jugs. In later years the baskets became collectors' items, highly prized by white settlers and, in modern times, by tourists.

The Southern Paiute had no central or political authority. Most bands did have a head man whose authority was more advisory than real. One famous *pak-winavi*—"big talker"—was "Chief" Tecopa, a regional leader with a reputation as a peacemaker. Tecopa, whose name means "wildcat," was born about 1815 and died in 1904; his lifetime spanned a period of tumultuous change for the Southern Paiutes.

The famous Southern Paiute "Chief" Tecopa (center) with two southern Nevada ranchers, circa 1900. Tecopa is said to have obtained his top hat and a bandmaster's uniform in exchange for showing a prominent Death Valley area mining man the location of a gold mine. University of Nevada, Las Vegas–Dickinson Library Special Collections

Two Southern Paiute brothers and their wives in 1873. The Southern Paiute Indians possessed a culture admirably suited to survival in the harsh southern Nevada desert environment. University of Nevada, Las Vegas–Dickinson Library Special Collections

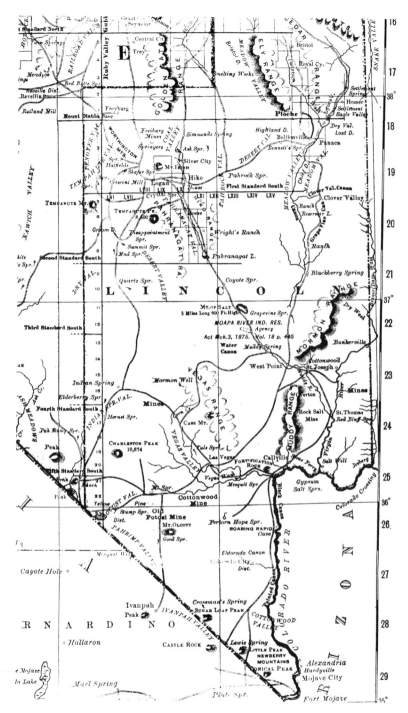

An 1881 map showing a relatively undeveloped southern Nevada. At this time Las Vegas was no more than the site of several ranches, and San Bernadino in the Los Angeles area was the nearest permanent community of any size. Much of the vast area between the 38th and 35th parallels in Nevada and eastern California was then relatively unexplored. University of Nevada, Las Vegas–Dickinson Library Special Collections

CHAPTER 2

Early Exploration

Until the middle of the nineteenth century, explorers generally avoided entering the vast inhospitable region that included most of the state of Nevada and the deserts of southwestern Utah and southern California.

Franciscan missionary Father Francisco Garces is usually credited with being the first person of European descent to enter what is now the state of Nevada. In the spring of 1776, while on one of his several scouting probes into the desert areas of southern California and Arizona, Garces may have ventured approximately into what is now Clark County, home of Las Vegas.

In 1829 a New Mexican merchant, Antonio Armijo, and his party left northern New Mexico and made their way through western Utah and southern Nevada. Armijo was one of the first persons of European descent to reach California from New Mexico, and his route became known as the Spanish Trail. While traveling east of the Las Vegas Valley as part of Armijo's expedition, Rafael Rivera, who was scouting ahead of the main party, became the first European to enter the Las Vegas Valley. Armijo's party is thought to have traveled up the Las Vegas Wash from the Colorado River and into the Las Vegas Valley, then south to the dry lake bed at Jean. They went to Goodsprings, crossed the Pahrump Valley, and on across the Mojave Desert to the Los Angeles basin.

The Spanish Trail established by Armijo became the preferred route from New Mexico to southern California, and over the next two decades large caravans wended their way along its sinuous path. Legitimate traders, thieves, and bands of raiders known as *los chaguanosos* ("the raiders") moved along the trail in both directions (Lingenfelter, 1986:25).

Colonel John Charles Fremont, the renowned American explorer and pathfinder. Between 1842 and 1854 Fremont made five expeditions into the Rocky Mountain West, accompanied by such fabled mountain men as Kit Carson, Joseph Walker, and Alexis Godey. Fremont camped at the Las Vegas Springs in 1844.
University of Nevada, Las Vegas–Dickinson Library
Special Collections

In the spring of 1844, John C. Fremont left southern California, heading for Kansas City. He was on his second expedition and in the company of scout Kit Carson. After a violent encounter between two of Fremont's men, Carson and Alex Godey, and Indians, south of Death Valley, the expedition traveled across Pahrump Valley and camped at Las Vegas Springs on the Spanish Trail. The springs, which were located not far from the present site of the Meadows Mall a few miles west of modern downtown Las Vegas, and lush meadows fed by the waters, located about 3 miles away, provided a welcome oasis for travelers crossing the valley.

After 1849 the eastern half of the Spanish Trail fell into disuse, and the portion from Nevada to California became linked with a trail to Salt Lake City. The new route became known as the Mormon Trail, or Mormon Road. The first wagon moved over this route in the winter of 1849–1850.

The Mormon Trail supported a brisk trade from 1855 to the turn of the century, when it was replaced by a railroad and, later, a highway. Las Vegas's location—at the approximate halfway point between Salt Lake City and southern California—and its water resources were to become key factors in the community's development.

The End of the Indian Way of Life

Indian contact with whites in southern Nevada was infrequent at first. Initially the Southern Paiute Indians only observed caravans and travelers as they passed through. Whites had few things that the Southern Paiute envied or desired, apart perhaps from cattle and horses. Although the Southern Paiute did not see any advantage to using horses for transporting goods or for riding, horses and cattle were sources of food, and attempts to steal them led to sporadic outbreaks of violence. As settlers began to occupy the Las Vegas Valley and construct homes near choice water sites, the natives sometimes found themselves in conflict with the settlers over ownership of the land and produce from gardens and fields.

During the second half of the nineteenth century, deprivation caused by fighting, white man's diseases, and disruption of the traditional Southern Paiute way of life took a terrible toll on the Southern Paiute population. By 1900 the number of Southern Paiute Indians in the Las Vegas area was only a fraction of what it had been before the arrival of the whites. Gradually the Indians found themselves enmeshed in white culture, working as laborers in mines and on the ranches and as domestic help on ranches and in towns. The vast area was no longer theirs to roam and use as they pleased.

Around 1900, it became clear to Helen Stewart, a pioneer rancher and the most prominent woman in Las Vegas at the time, that the Southern Paiute in Las Vegas needed a home that no one could take from them. In 1911, she deeded ten acres of her ranch for their use. In 1912, the U.S. government paid Stewart $500 and formally accepted the land, which lay just north of the growing community of Las Vegas and which is now known as the Las Vegas Colony. In 1926, about fifty Paiute made their headquarters there and supported themselves by working as laborers in the area.

The Mormon Mission of 1855

Mormon colonists settled in the Salt Lake area in 1847. Between then and the spring of 1855, a score of Mormon communities were founded between Salt Lake City and Cedar City, Utah, to provide homes for new immigrants, to raise crops, and to establish a line of way stations on the Mormon Trail between the Salt Lake Valley and the religious group's settlement in San Bernardino, California.

In April 1855, Brigham Young, head of the Mormon Church, announced that a mission would be established in the Las Vegas Valley, then part of the New Mexico Territory. On June 14 of that year a party of thirty missionaries and forty ox-drawn wagons arrived in the valley and selected a site about 4 miles east of the Las Vegas Springs. The missionaries cleared the land of mesquite and brush and planted crops (alfalfa, squash, potatoes, beans, melons, grain, and turnips) and fruit trees, and they began the construction of the Las Vegas Fort. Today this site is at the southeast corner of Las Vegas Boulevard and Washington Avenue.

Under the leadership of William Bringhurst, the missionaries were determined to develop good relations with the Indians and attempted to convert them

William Bringhurst, leader of the 1855 Mormon mission to the Las Vegas Valley. Photo taken in the 1850s. University of Nevada , Las Vegas–Dickinson Library Special Collections

to the Mormon faith. Some Indians were baptized as Mormons and were given Christian names.

In January 1856, church authorities issued a call for more missionaries to go to Las Vegas. Twenty-six men responded, and several brought their families. In August of that year, the wife of one of these men gave birth to Zelpha Daedura Fuller, the first white child born at the fort.

In 1856 a deposit of lead ore bearing significant quantities of silver and zinc was discovered on the west side of Mount Potosi, located about 20 miles southwest of Las Vegas. The Mormons, who had difficulty farming in the alkaline soil, turned part of their attention to mining, with minimal success. Divided attention, combined with the Indians' constant theft of animals and food and the intermittent, sometimes serious, bickering among the missionaries, led church authorities to abandon the unsuccessful mission in February 1857. Some volunteers remained, but by the fall of 1858 all missionary activity had ceased.

Once the mission was deserted, the roof burned and the adobe walls began to erode. Travelers used the walls as corrals and carried off anything of value. For a short time in the early 1860s, Albert Knapp, one of the original members of the Las Vegas Mission, operated a store at the site. But by 1865, the fort was largely in ruins. Meanwhile, news of gold and silver in the desert was spreading.

Potosi Mine, located high on the slopes of the west side of Mount Potosi, approximately 30 miles southwest of Las Vegas. Local Indians first showed the Mormons the mine's location in the spring of 1856; the missionaries worked the large deposit of lead, zinc, and silver ore with only modest success. In 1861, after the Mormons had abandoned their mission, the mine was the site of a small boom. There was speculation that the mine would rival the Comstock Lode, but this never proved to be the case. The mine has been operated at various times since then, including during World War I, when it was active in producing zinc and lead for the war effort. University of Nevada, Las Vegas–Dickinson Library Special Collections

Sketch of the Stewart Ranch by artist and photographer Frederick S. Dellenbaugh, March 16, 1876. The building with two windows in the foreground was constructed by Mormon missionaries. The Mormons abandoned the mission in 1858, after which it was occupied by Octavius Decatur Gass. He built the property up and remained there from 1865 to 1881, when it was acquired by Pioche rancher Archibald Stewart. Most travelers crossing the Las Vegas Valley stopped at the ranch. University of Nevada, Las Vegas–Dickinson Library Special Collections

The Stewart Ranch, circa 1900. Nepwork Photos

In the Aftermath of the Gold Diggers: The Valley Is Settled

Europeans and frontiersmen journeyed throughout the West for many years before they began to fully appreciate the enormous mineral wealth contained in its streams and mountains. Small deposits of placer gold were found in southern California at various times between 1775 and 1828, and in 1838 placers were discovered 45 miles north of Los Angeles and worked for twenty years. The stampede of wealth seekers was finally triggered by the discovery of gold near Sutter's Fort in northern California in 1848. Those that reached the California goldfields too late to cash in spilled over into nearby areas, including what was to become Nevada. After a party of gold seekers narrowly escaped with their lives in 1849 after attempting a shortcut to California across Death Valley, legends began to spread of fabulous lost gold and silver mines on the desert.

The First Ranches in Las Vegas

The first permanent settlements in the Las Vegas Valley owe their birth to mining. Prior to 1858, mining in the Las Vegas area consisted of sporadic activity at the Mormons' Potosi lead mine and at claims staked by itinerant prospectors in the El Dorado Canyon area, located about 40 miles southeast of Las Vegas on the Colorado River. By the early 1860s, between 300 and 500 people were working in the Colorado mining district, as the El Dorado Canyon area was known. The miners needed food and supplies, and others who saw opportunity came to occupy land in the Las Vegas Valley.

In late 1865 Octavius Decatur (O. D.) Gass, a native of Ohio and a miner, and two partners claimed the Las Vegas Fort property. They repaired the buildings,

Octavius Decatur Gass, circa 1885.
Nepwork Photos

Helen J. Stewart, circa 1885. A diminutive woman described as a "tiny Dresden China piece of femininity" (C. M. Townley, 1973:26–27), she was pregnant with her fifth child when her husband was killed by gunfire on the Kiel Ranch in 1884. In 1916 she became the first woman elected to the Clark County School Board. University of Nevada, Las Vegas–Dickinson Library Special Collections

rebuilt fences and irrigation ditches, and began planting crops. By 1871 about 150 acres were in cultivation. Each year the acreage produced two crops plus a variety of fruit. Grain, including wheat, barley, and oats, was harvested in the late spring, and then such foods as corn, potatoes, beets, cabbage, onions, and squash were planted. Local Indians provided most of the labor, and travelers on the Mormon Trail and miners at El Dorado Canyon and boom camps across the California border provided the market. Pound for pound, the prices obtained from farm products often exceeded the value of the miners' ore.

By the late 1870s Gass had acquired a number of adjacent ranch properties and controlled nearly all of the valuable agricultural land in the area. Among his purchases was the ranch at Big Springs that had been established by James B. Wilson and his partner, John Howell, the first known black resident of the valley. Not long after Gass purchased these properties, he tried to sell his ranch, now known as the Las Vegas Ranch, but he found no takers. Using his ranch as collateral in 1879, Gass borrowed $5,000 from Archibald Stewart, a mining and ranching man from Pioche, Nevada. Monthly interest was 2.5 percent, and the loan was to be repaid in one year. A second loan was obtained from Stewart to repay the first. Gass failed to repay the second note and Stewart took possession by foreclosure. Gass and his family continued to live on the ranch until June 1881, when they departed for southern California.

Archibald Stewart, his wife, Helen, and their three children took up residence at the Las Vegas Ranch in April 1882. Soon thereafter, Stewart began selling his produce at El Dorado Canyon. He and a ranch hand would take two wagons to El Dorado Canyon, leaving the ranch in the early evening. The next morning they would reach the canyon, where they sold fresh alfalfa, fruit, vegetables, and beef. The men would rest until evening and then begin their journey back to the ranch. Although Stewart was a successful businessman, his "cold and calculating methods" made him unpopular with those with whom he did business (C. M. Townley, 1973:220).

During this period Conrad Kiel operated the only other ranch of consequence in the Las Vegas Valley. Kiel and O. D. Gass may have been neighbors in Ohio. Kiel looked up his old friend Gass when he arrived in the valley and for a time worked on Gass's ranch.

Remains of the Mormon fort as it appeared circa 1940. Portions of the adobe structure that the Mormon missionaries originally constructed were still standing. University of Nevada, Las Vegas–Dickinson Library Special Collections

Interior of Helen Stewart's adobe home located at the site of the old Mormon fort on the Stewart Ranch, circa 1909. The dog on the sofa appears to be the one in the photo on page 12. The fine Indian baskets above the fireplace were part of Helen Stewart's collection, for which she was widely known.
University of Nevada, Las Vegas–Dickinson Library Special Collections

Unidentified man with horses and fruit wagon belonging to the Kiel Ranch, circa 1910.
University of Nevada, Las Vegas–Dickinson Library Special Collections

The history of the Kiel Ranch (now known as the Kyle Ranch) dates to 1875, when Conrad Kiel filed on undeveloped land featuring a spring located about 1½ miles north of the fort. He built an adobe cabin, ran cattle, and farmed the site. He also operated a small store on the ranch, selling tobacco, tools, and wagon supplies to local residents and travelers. Kiel was joined in the venture by his son Edwin. The Kiels were hard workers but were not considered good farmers. They did have considerable skill, however, in growing grapes, and the wines they produced were renowned. The elder Kiel also operated a sawmill in the Charleston Mountains, and lumber from his mill was used in the construction of many of the first buildings in the Las Vegas Valley.

Kiel's ranch became known as a hangout for toughs and lawbreakers. Gunfights were apparently common, and outlaws and desert frontiersmen such as the notorious killer Hank Parish and legendary gunslinger Jack Longstreet were often found there. The ranch soon had a reputation as the scene of not one, but two bloody shootouts.

Murder on the Kiel Ranch

During the summer of 1884, the Stewarts employed a man named Schyler Henry. In July of that year, while Archibald Stewart was away, Henry suddenly quit. He turned up on the Kiel Ranch, where he allegedly spread malicious gossip regarding Stewart's wife, Helen.

When Stewart returned to his ranch, Helen informed him of Henry's activities. That afternoon Stewart took his rifle and rode to the Kiel Ranch. According to Henry's testimony, he was inside the ranch house—the ranch was apparently otherwise deserted—when through a window he saw Archibald Stewart walking toward the house, rifle in hand. Henry reached for a shotgun, found it unloaded, and ran toward a Spencer rifle at the other window. Stewart fired at Henry and missed. When Henry moved behind the door, Stewart held his gun against it and fired. The bullet grazed Henry's arm. Stewart and Henry then fired almost simultaneously. Henry received a flesh wound in the hip; Stewart was hit in the chest. Henry then shot Stewart in the head.

Edwin and William Kiel, sons of Conrad Kiel, owner of the Kiel Ranch located in present-day North Las Vegas, circa 1885. University of Nevada, Las Vegas–Dickinson Library Special Collections

Conrad Kiel found Stewart later that day and sent a terse note to Helen Stewart: "Mrs. Stewart, Send a team and take Mr. Stewart away he is dead. C. Kiel" (Stewart, 1884).

A grand jury investigated Stewart's murder. Having only Henry's account of the gunfight, the jury ruled that Henry had killed Stewart in self-defense.

Helen Stewart never accepted the grand jury's decision. She believed that Henry, Hank Parish, and Conrad Kiel were involved in a plot to kill her husband, but she was never able to prove her assertions. Perhaps Kiel may have resented the manner in which Stewart had acquired the ranch from his old friend, Gass.

The intrigue did not end with Archibald Stewart's death. In April 1900 Edwin Kiel was joined at the ranch by his brother, William. On October 11 Helen and Archibald's son, Will, and the foreman of the Stewart Ranch, Frank Stewart (no relation to the Stewarts, although he later married Helen), went to the Kiel Ranch to pay a visit and to replenish their supply of tobacco.

When the men arrived at the ranch they found the front and back doors of the house ajar. They could see Edwin Kiel's body on the kitchen floor and a pistol, which was lying near his right hand. Thirty feet from the house they discovered the body of William Kiel partly submerged in an irrigation ditch with a double-barreled shotgun at his feet. There were no witnesses. The coroner's jury concluded that Edwin Kiel had killed William and then, in remorse, shot himself.

Although the verdict stood through the years, many people wondered about the shootings. In the mid-1970s, researchers at the University of Nevada, Las Vegas, exhumed the remains of the Kiel brothers. Forensic analysis of their remains suggested that the coroner's jury had erred. The researchers concluded that it had not been a murder-suicide, but a double murder: Edwin Kiel had died from a bullet wound not to the front of the face, but to the back of the head.

Who killed the Kiel brothers? Could it have been members of the Stewart family who sought revenge for Archibald Stewart's death? The events will probably remain a mystery forever.

The Railroad Makes Plans for the Valley

At the turn of the century, Salt Lake City was the largest city between the Rocky Mountains and the West Coast. Salt Lake was linked by rail on the New York–Chicago–San Francisco trade route, but there was no rail link to the south, connecting the city with the growing southern California area. Surveys established that the most cost-efficient route to southern California would roughly follow the old Mormon Trail along a line of interconnected valleys. The Las Vegas Valley was propitiously located near the midpoint of this line, and it was especially attractive because of its abundant water supplies.

Rumors of a railroad circulated in the Las Vegas Valley for several years after 1900. The rumors would surface and strangers would appear, then vanish; sometimes a surveyor with chain and tripod would be seen, only to disappear like the others. The smell of opportunity drew people—including the ubiquitous gamblers—to the area. The planned construction of such a railroad eventually led to the founding of the city of Las Vegas.

Two giants of American industry vied for the right to construct the railroad that would link Salt Lake and southern California: Edward H. Harriman, who controlled the Union Pacific Railroad, and Montana copper king Senator William A. Clark. The Union Pacific was the first on the scene. By 1889, Union Pacific had acquired a number of short-line railroads in Utah, which were consolidated and commonly referred to as the Oregon Short Line. By 1899 trains were in operation from Salt Lake City to the Utah-Nevada border west of Cedar City, Utah.

Much to the consternation of Harriman and Union Pacific officials, in 1900 Senator Clark, a newcomer to the railroad business, jumped in. He purchased the Los Angeles Terminal Railroad and a Utah railroad that had, until he purchased it, existed only on paper. Clark then pushed forward to construct his own line, the San Pedro, Los Angeles, and Salt Lake Railroad (SP, LA, & SL Railroad). Clark's and Harriman's interests eventually collided over the right to lay tracks down the Meadow Valley Wash, about 150 miles north of Las Vegas. Both groups thought this route was the best way to connect the higher elevations on the Utah border to the lower desert of southern Nevada. The Clark-Harriman War, as it was known, was eventually resolved when Union Pacific acquired a fifty-percent interest in Clark's railroad company.

In the fall of 1902 Clark purchased most of the Las Vegas Ranch from Helen Stewart for $55,000. The sale included 1,800 acres of land, the ranch house and buildings, and all the water from the Las Vegas Springs. To solidify his grip on land holdings in the Las Vegas Valley, Clark also purchased the Kyle (Kiel) Ranch and its springs.

The first train ran from Salt Lake City to Los Angeles by way of the old Stewart Ranch on February 9, 1905, and the line was considered formally open for business on May 1 of that year.

Officials of the San Pedro, Los Angeles, and Salt Lake Railroad had a railroad car moved alongside the railroad tracks across Main Street at the head of Fremont Street, where it was used as Las Vegas's first train depot prior to construction of a permanent depot at the site. The Union Plaza Hotel now stands at the location. University of Nevada, Las Vegas–Dickinson Library Special Collections

The Clark townsite land auction, May 15, 1905. Bidders stood in the hot sun (the temperature was over 100 degrees) waiting for their opportunity to purchase lots in the new townsite. University of Nevada, Las Vegas–Dickinson Library Special Collections

CHAPTER 4

The Town Is Born

By the summer of 1904 the construction of the railroad grade for Clark's line in the Las Vegas Valley was under way. Everyone knew there was going to be a town in the Las Vegas Valley. The only question was where it would be located. Senator Clark had acquired the best of the land and water resources with the purchase of the Stewart and Kiel ranches. But J. T. McWilliams, a well-known area surveyor who had earlier surveyed the Stewart Ranch for Helen Stewart, saw an opportunity. He filed for a quarter section of land that adjoined the Stewart Ranch on the north and west. The railroad survey showed that the tracks would shave a bit off a corner of his property. McWilliams shrewdly parceled his land and began selling lots adjoining the tracks. He named the subdivision the "Original Townsite of Las Vegas" (Squires and Squires, 1955:209). To sell his lots he ran advertisements in Los Angeles's daily newspapers.

The Rise and Fall of McWilliams's Townsite

As work on the railroad progressed, McWilliams's townsite became a lively town with a well-established business district comprising three or four tent saloons, a lodging house, and several stores. A number of large corrals housed the many horses and mules used in the area's active freighting business. The community prospered, supported mainly by the drivers and hustlers of the freight teams.

Life in the tent town was crude and harsh, particularly in the winter. Canvas hotels offered rooms with no heat, and strong winds blew straight through the fabric. The tent saloons were especially popular for they offered warmth as well as whiskey and gambling.

Six mules, known as a "three span," heading for Beatty, Nevada, with a water wagon, circa 1905.
University of Nevada, Las Vegas–Dickinson Library Special Collections

Although many thought that McWilliams's townsite would be the heart of Las Vegas, others realized that the railroad also planned to sell lots alongside the new line. After the railroad held its auction on May 15, 1905, the population of McWilliams's townsite rapidly dwindled. The end came on the evening of September 5, 1905, when a fire started under suspicious conditions and the town was largely destroyed.

Nevertheless, despite the demise of McWilliams's town, the site remained a thriving supply center. The discovery of a huge deposit of silver ore 210 miles to the north in 1900 led to the immediate development of the town of Tonopah. In 1902 an immense gold deposit was found 26 miles south of Tonopah at Goldfield; fortune seekers rushed to the area. Two years later prospectors found gold at Rhyolite, just 120 miles north of Las Vegas. By 1909, Goldfield, Tonopah, Reno, and Rhyolite were, in that order, the four largest communities in the state of Nevada. Las Vegas was a vital supply center for all those communities but Reno.

Clark's Townsite Auction

The beginning of the town of Las Vegas—the point when it became more than an assemblage of small ranches and a speculative townsite—is usually dated to the townsite auction held by officials of Clark's San Pedro, Los Angeles, and Salt Lake Railroad on May 15, 1905. It was then that what is now downtown Las Vegas was first established.

A great deal of excitement was generated by the proposed sale of lots at the Clark townsite, located just south and east of McWilliams's townsite. Five days before lots were to be sold, 3,000 applications had been filed with the claims agent. Demand for lots was so strong that railroad officials announced that the lots would be sold at auction. When the sale opened on May 15, 3,000 speculators were present. Many were from Los Angeles and Salt Lake City and had arrived on special excursion trains, paying round-trip fares of $16 and $20—hefty sums in those days. The bidding in the hot sun on the first day of the auction was fierce, and lots on Fremont Street between Main and First streets sold for $750, $800, and $850.

Building was already under way by the end of the auction's first day. Tent houses and shacks on drays or skids were pulled to the lots from all directions, their progress marked by great pillars of dust rising in the sky. The sounds of saws and hammers drowned out conversation. By morning of the next day new establishments were open for business.

Block 16 of the townsite was lined with saloons and gambling clubs, pictured here in 1906. With its boisterous and ribald image, Block 16 helped set the tone of Las Vegas's future development.
Nepwork Photos

Block 16: Where the Good Times Rolled

Early Las Vegas was a man's town filled with miners, teamsters, prospectors, drifters, and any manner of humanity in search of a fast buck. Yet, odd as it may seem, Las Vegas actually began as a temperance town. A "no liquor" clause was written into the deeds of the lots sold at the Clark townsite. Exceptions were made for hotels, drug stores, establishments serving liquor with meals, doctors' prescriptions, and Blocks 16 and 17, between First and Third streets on Ogden and Stewart streets.

Although the railroad's exclusionary liquor rules were challenged in court and never really enforced (they were not stricken from the titles until 1948), they had the effect of forming social boundaries within the new community. Before the end of 1905, Block 16 on north First Street on the east side of the street between Ogden and Stewart streets became widely known as a red-light district, and it was as tough as the most boisterous of the 1870s western mining towns. Riots, shootings, and fights erupted continually.

The entire block was filled with saloons and gambling clubs with names such as the Gem, the Red Onion, and the Double-O. These establishments welcomed their wild, fun-seeking clientele day and night, dispensing whiskey and offering gambling, eager to relieve any patron of his paycheck.

The Arizona Club was considered the high-class establishment on Block 16, and it became a rendezvous for railroad passengers drawn by Block 16's widely known reputation. The club, which opened on March 31, 1906, was elaborately furnished by its owner, J. C. "Jim" McIntosh. The front doors boasted beveled glass and fancy fittings, and the bar featured carved red mahogany columns, marble baseboards, and mahogany wainscoting and was illuminated by gaslight. Drinks were fifteen cents; a sloe gin fizz was the house specialty. Faro, roulette, and blackjack tables stood alongside nickel slot machines.

Freight wagons and teams on Block 16, Las Vegas, Nevada, circa early 1907, probably headed for Rhyolite gold camp. Note the Arizona Club in the background. Nepwork Photos

The Arizona Club, circa 1910. The simple frame structure shown in the previous photos was rebuilt with brick and quickly became the "class" of Block 16. University of Nevada, Las Vegas–Dickinson Library Special Collections

LAS VEGAS

The activities on Block 16 were tolerated by the community. Prostitution was permitted on the east side of Block 16, and women other than prostitutes and those of compromised reputation were not allowed in the bars. As long as they behaved themselves, the prostitutes were permitted to patronize the banks, movie theaters, dress shops, and mercantile stores; the cash they used for payment was always welcome. Prostitutes received weekly medical examinations by selected local physicians and enjoyed the protection of the law.

Years later—in 1942, as a result of protests from the U.S. Army and finagling by local businessmen who were trying to buy the Block 16 property for a low price—the notorious establishments were shut down. But the legacy of Block 16 is apparent today: In many ways, modern Las Vegas owes much to that boisterous and ribald district.

The Arizona Club was famous for its bar, which, with fittings, is thought to have cost more than $20,000. The bar was moved to the Last Frontier's Horn Room in 1942. University of Nevada, Las Vegas–Dickinson Library Special Collections

Two prostitutes sitting in front of the Arizona Club, circa 1932. In 1912, the Arizona Club was sold and the new owner added a second story to the building, offering a new service—the "ladies upstairs." University of Nevada, Las Vegas–Dickinson Library Special Collections

The city's hotels had humble beginnings: Pictured here is the Hotel Las Vegas, completed by May 14, 1905. The hotel was located a block and a half north of Fremont on Main Street.

University of Nevada, Las Vegas–Dickinson Library Special Collections

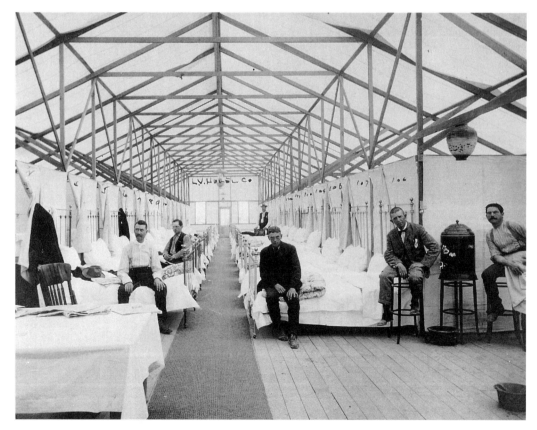

Interior of the Las Vegas Hotel, 1905. All the hotel's furnishings were shipped in on the railroad prior to the Clark land auction. University of Nevada, Las Vegas–Dickinson Library Special Collections

The Town's First Hotels

The first hotel in Las Vegas opened for business on February 13, 1905. Known as Ladd's Hotel, it was one in a row of small tents that stretched diagonally through the sagebrush toward a point near what is now Main and Carson streets. Ladd's Hotel was only 12 feet by 20 feet with just four double beds, each of which accommodated two persons for an eight-hour shift. The proprietor, Captain James H. Ladd, had one steadfast rule: "If you scratch you get no bed in this hotel." Ladd kept potential patrons waiting so that he could observe whether they scratched; if they did, they slept elsewhere (Squires and Squires, 1955:412).

Longtime Las Vegas resident C. P. "Pop" Squires opened the Hotel Las Vegas three months later, on May 14, 1905, the day before the Clark land auction. Although it, too, was a tent, it was much more luxurious. Its components were precut in Los Angeles and shipped by railroad to Las Vegas, where they were assembled.

The Hotel Las Vegas boasted a plank floor and a front porch. The main part, which measured 40 by 130 feet, was divided by canvas partitions into a front lobby, thirty rooms, and a dormitory. Another tent was used as a dining room; behind that stood the kitchen tent. Each room was furnished with an iron and copper bedstead, chair, washbowl, chamber pot, and pitcher; there was no plumbing. A bright metal bracket holding a drinking glass added a "touch of elegance" to each room (Squires and Squires, 1955:306). The hotel was dismantled in early 1906.

The Community Grows—Slowly

Tents gradually gave way to homes and stores of frame and concrete block construction; by 1908 Las Vegas boasted many permanent buildings and had graded and oiled streets, wooden and concrete curbs, and a volunteer fire department. Electricity was supplied by a subsidiary of the railroad, but power was unavailable during the day until 1915, when the first 24-hour service was established.

Union Station at the head of Fremont Street, Las Vegas, Nevada, circa 1908. Nepwork Photos

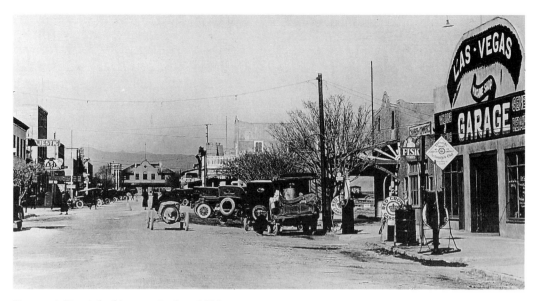

Fremont Street, looking west, circa 1915. University of Nevada, Las Vegas–Dickinson Library Special Collections

For the first fifteen years of its life, Las Vegas remained small and isolated—and very much dependent on the railroad. This dependency was apparent each time a flood washed out the railroad tracks. In 1910 a great flood destroyed more than 110 miles of track in Meadow Valley Wash to the north. It was months before the line could be repaired, and the town of Las Vegas fell into a depression for the first half of the year.

Early boosters promoted the abundance of land and water; there were even high hopes for the valley's agricultural opportunities. In 1913 the mayor of Las Vegas, Peter Buol, recruited investors from Scotland to develop farms in the Las Vegas Valley. Community members envisioned the entire valley covered with picturesque and highly productive farms, but the hard alkaline soil proved unfavorable, and the agricultural ventures were soon abandoned.

The Strong-Minded People of North Las Vegas

The community of North Las Vegas, which today includes the site of the old Kiel Ranch, was founded in 1917 by Tom Williams, who had moved to Las Vegas from Utah. Williams purchased 140 acres located about a mile north of the Clark townsite. He kept 40 acres for himself and subdivided the balance. He envisioned a community made up of "strong-minded people" who would not impose business licenses or other kinds of restrictions on its residents. People who felt crowded in the small—some said "stuffy"—community of Las Vegas saw the new town as a place for expansion and freedom (Lewis, 1976).

The character of the young community was further shaped by the passage of the Volstead Act in 1919, enacting Prohibition. Las Vegas adhered somewhat to the act and on occasion prosecuted producers of alcoholic beverages. Many of the violators moved north; 31 of the first 80 lots sold by Williams were bought by bootleggers, who constructed their homes over huge basements outfitted with distillery equipment. Speakeasies were abundant, and local legend maintains that a complex of tunnels ran from one bar to another beneath the town's main thoroughfares.

By the end of the 1920s other land developers saw opportunities in "North Town," as the community was sometimes called. In 1932 a post office was established with the name North Las Vegas, but only after first being called Vegas Verde for two months.

Grapevines, Kiel Ranch, located in present-day North Las Vegas, Nevada, 1919. From the time of its occupation by Conrad Kiel in the 1870s, the Kiel Ranch was known for the quality and vintage of its grapes.
University of Nevada, Las Vegas–Dickinson Library Special Collections

City limits of North Las Vegas, circa 1949, looking north on Main Street. Nepwork Photos

In the 1920s: Not a Roar but a Whimper

Las Vegas's dependency on the railroad persisted throughout the 1920s. In 1921 Union Pacific assumed control of Senator Clark's holdings in the SP, LA, & SL Railroad. In a departure from the senator's paternalistic attitude toward the small desert town, officials discharged sixty employees without explanation from the Las Vegas repair facility. In 1922 Las Vegas workers participated enthusiastically in the great nationwide railroad strike. Scabs were brought into Las Vegas, and violence flared. Tracks were closed for several weeks, and the town's economy suffered. In a vindictive mood when the strike was over, Union Pacific moved the repair shop to Caliente. The closure meant the loss of 300 jobs and was a bitter blow to the town.

Through it all, though, Las Vegas survived and even grew. In 1920 its population was 2,304, and by 1930 it had grown to 5,165. By the mid-1920s Las Vegas had two banks, five churches, and two newspapers. Yet, with limited agricultural potential, lack of mines and industry, and loss of railroad jobs, residents knew their future depended on attracting others to their desert oasis.

In the 1920s Las Vegas was successful in its efforts to route a highway connecting Los Angeles and Salt Lake City through town. By 1927 more than 450 cars were passing through Las Vegas each day.

The town's first airport, Rockwell Field, was completed in 1921. The field was located about 3 miles south of town, approximately where the Sahara's parking lot is today.

A native of Blythe, California, flying a DeHavilland Jenny in the spring of 1920, is credited with the Las Vegas Valley's first recorded flight. Airmail service between Los Angeles and Salt Lake City, with Las Vegas as a refueling point, began in April 1926; passenger service out of Las Vegas began a month later, on May 23, 1926, when Western Air Express began carrying its first passengers in M-2 biplanes covered with red canvas. The round-trip fare between Los Angeles and Las Vegas was $80. In 1929 Western Air Express, which had outgrown the facilities at Rockwell Field, moved to a site north of town occupied today by Nellis Air Force Base.

Fremont Street, looking east, 1921, after a rare snowstorm. Golden Hotel is on the right.
University of Nevada, Las Vegas–Dickinson Library Special Collections

Las Vegas's first airfield was constructed in 1921 at the intersection of two dirt roads—San Francisco Street (now Sahara Avenue) and Paradise Road, located approximately where the Sahara Hotel's parking lot is today. Pictured here are the airport office and a windsock used to indicate wind velocity and direction. Known as Rockwell Field, the airport was named after the owner of the land, Leon Rockwell. Nepwork Photos

Fremont Street, looking east, circa 1925. At center is the Northern Club, which received the first gaming license in Las Vegas when gambling was legalized in Nevada in 1931. Though gambling was illegal when this photo was taken, few people were deterred from frequenting the clubs. Nepwork Photos

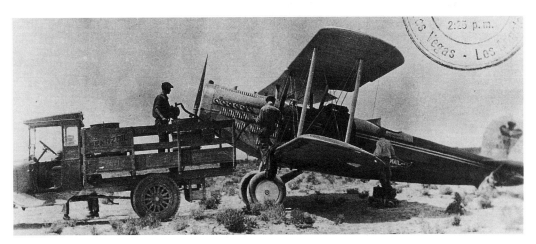

Contract airmail service between Los Angeles, Las Vegas, and Salt Lake City was inaugurated April 17, 1926. A Douglas M-2 airplane is pictured being refueled at Rockwell Field.
University of Nevada, Las Vegas–Dickinson Library Special Collections

It had long been recognized that the great canyon holding the Colorado River east of Las Vegas was a wonderful site for a large dam. Here, workers are digging in the riverbed of the Colorado River, preparing a foundation for Hoover Dam in April 1933. Water from the river was diverted around the construction site by means of an upstream coffer dam and tunnels through the canyon walls. Looking downstream, the lower coffer dam is visible. U.S. Bureau of Reclamation

CHAPTER 5

Dams, Dice, and Divorce: Las Vegas in the 1930s

The 1930s were kind to Las Vegas and the surrounding region. Most of the town's growth in that decade was the result of a modern technical marvel: Hoover Dam. The potential for constructing a great dam in the canyon carved by the Colorado River to the east of Las Vegas had long been recognized, but private efforts to develop the site were unsuccessful. It took the resources of the federal government to do the job. Legislation authorizing the construction of Hoover Dam (the Boulder Canyon Project Act) was passed in 1928, triggering an economic boom in Las Vegas that essentially has not stopped to this day.

The Building of Boulder Dam

The first individual to seriously pursue the construction of a dam was Henry C. Schmidt, a Tonopah businessman. In 1910 Schmidt surveyed the dam site and filed an application with the U.S. Department of the Interior and the states of Nevada and Arizona for a permit to build a dam and a power plant at Boulder Canyon. Permits were promptly granted, and investors were found for the company, called the Colorado River Power Company. Work on the dam was scheduled to begin in October 1914, but those plans were abandoned when World War I broke out in Europe. Although Schmidt attempted to keep his permit alive, it was canceled in 1922.

Powerful agriculture and public utility forces in southern California had also become interested in constructing a dam on the Colorado River. Initial thinking was focused on constructing a dam to control flooding below Las Vegas, but as sites for construction were surveyed, the project became more than an irrigation

Hoover Dam as seen from the cableway stretching across the Black Canyon, December 1933. U.S. Bureau of Reclamation

President Franklin Delano Roosevelt dedicating Boulder (Hoover) Dam, September 30 1935. Eleanor Roosevelt (white hat) is sitting just behind the president. U.S. Bureau of Reclamation

effort, and the dam's potential to generate electricity was considered. Seventy sites were narrowed to five, including Black Canyon and nearby Boulder Canyon; eventually Black Canyon became the designated site because of its superior rock formation and the need to construct the shortest possible railroad line from Las Vegas (but Boulder Canyon's name stuck to the project).

The construction of Hoover Dam—or Boulder Dam, as it was then known—began in March 1931. It was the largest building project in the western hemisphere following the completion of the Panama Canal. Fifty-two miles of railroad were built to supply construction material to the site. Before construction of the dam began, tunnels were built to divert the river around the dam site and a temporary dam above the dam site was constructed. The first concrete at the dam site was poured on June 6, 1933.

On February 1, 1935, water was impounded behind the unfinished dam. The last concrete was poured on May 29, 1935, and on September 30, President Franklin D. Roosevelt dedicated the dam. At the ceremony, Roosevelt designated the dam Boulder Dam, officially dropping Hoover as its name. In 1947, the Republican-controlled Congress acted to change the dam's name back to Hoover Dam.

Hoover Dam contains 3,220,000 cubic yards of concrete and stands 727 feet high. At its crest it is 45 feet thick and 1,244 feet in length; it is 660 feet thick at its base. By 1939, the dam was putting out the equivalent of 1,835,000 horsepower, about 64 percent of which went to California, with Nevada and Arizona splitting the remainder.

When cheap electricity became available from Hoover Dam, the use of swamp coolers and, later, air conditioners to moderate the hot summer temperatures in the Las Vegas Valley became a major factor in the city's growth.

Aerial view of Hoover Dam, 1978. Just seven years transpired from the dam's authorization to its dedication—a remarkable feat of engineering and labor. Nepwork Photos

Shanty constructed of mud and canvas, Las Vegas, circa 1930. Nepwork Photos

Thousands of jobless workers and their families flocked to the Las Vegas area during the Great Depression with hopes of working on the Boulder (Hoover) Dam. Pictured here are women and their children and the makeshift shelter they were forced to call home during the early 1930s.

U.S. Bureau of Reclamation

Aerial view of Boulder City, Nevada, looking north, 1934. U.S. Bureau of Reclamation Headquarters are in the large white building in the center of the photo. U.S. Bureau of Reclamation

LAS VEGAS

Sun City and the Model Community

Passage of the Boulder Canyon Project Act by Congress in 1928 received national attention and drew workers from around the country. With millions out of work during the Great Depression, the opportunity for jobs in Las Vegas was a clarion call to the unemployed. Shantytowns, known as Hoovervilles, sprang up a few blocks north of Las Vegas's business district, in North Las Vegas, and along the Colorado River. Most families lived in severe poverty, some even living in their cars. In one year, 1930, the population of Las Vegas grew from 5,200 to 7,500.

Initially Las Vegas promoters were hopeful that dam workers would be housed in Las Vegas, but the Department of Interior officials announced that a model community would be constructed near the dam site. Las Vegas's sinful image, based largely on the drinking, gambling, and prostitution on Block 16, undoubtedly influenced the decision. Officials cited their concern that bootleggers and other violators of the law might interfere with workers' lives.

Although Las Vegas did not get to house the workers, it did see that they were properly entertained. Establishments in Las Vegas offered workers a good time, guaranteeing them a wild and noisy night for a portion of their paycheck. It was said that lines of men formed in two places on payday: the Western Union office and the houses of prostitution.

Boulder City was a planned community designed for an initial 5,000 persons, with a permanent settlement of about 1,500. The desert heat was a major consideration in determining the town's location: Boulder City sits 8 miles from the dam, at a spot 2,000 feet higher—and noticeably cooler—than the dam vicinity. The government initially planned to build Boulder City in advance of the dam's construction, but because of the depression the construction schedule for the dam was moved forward, and the dam and town were begun at about the same time.

Auto court, Boulder City, Nevada, circa 1935. U.S. Bureau of Reclamation

Eight two-story dormitories, each housing 172 men, were constructed; surplus cottages from the 1932 Olympic Games were trucked in from Los Angeles for workers with families. By the end of 1932 all buildings on the project had electric coolers or air conditioners run by electricity from San Bernardino, 222 miles away. Plans for Boulder City included a hospital, general store, recreation hall, and commissary. Rent ranged from $15 a month for a one-room cottage for married couples to $30 a month for a three-room house. By 1932 the town had its own school, police station, post office, train station, and cemetery. Boulder City remained a federal town until 1960, when it was incorporated.

As homes and buildings in Boulder City were completed, the residents of the Las Vegas shanty towns who were employed at the dam moved in. Sims Ely, the autocratic city manager of Boulder City from 1931 to 1941, banished drunks and other unsuitable workers—he decided who could stay in Boulder City.

Many workers remained in the area after the dam was completed, wanting to capitalize on the promising tourist trade. Nearly 100,000 visitors had come to see the dam in 1932, while it was under construction; the figure ballooned to 265,000 in 1934. Las Vegas billed itself as "the gateway to the Hoover Dam," and the majority of those who came to see the dam also stopped in Las Vegas.

Fremont Street, looking west, circa 1935. Nepwork Photos

Earning Its Reputation

Writers who came to Las Vegas during the boom years of the 1930s to tell the story of the dam and the nearby community generally wrote about a wild frontier town where alcohol, prostitution, quick marriage and divorce, and gambling were readily available. These stories promoted Las Vegas's image as a place where fun and flirtation with immorality were possible without causing real harm to anyone. This image persisted and engendered the spirit by which the city and its reputation would grow.

During Prohibition (1919–1933) Las Vegas resisted compliance with the national laws to the best of its ability. To get around the "no liquor" clause that affected all establishments in the Clark townsite apart from those on Block 16, many establishments on Fremont Street simply added a couple of rooms and contended that they were hotels; they could thus serve alcohol. Local dispensers of alcoholic beverages nearly always received advance warning of visits from federal agents. Occasional arrests were necessary for the sake of appearances. Those who had been "caught" received small ritual fines but were usually back in business within days.

As for prostitution, it was both available and legal in Las Vegas. The brothels were licensed and regulated by city officials, including the City Council and the chief of police, and were as much a part of life in Las Vegas as they were in most frontier communities in the West. The brothels were located on First Street between Ogden and Stewart streets.

Getting married had always been easy in Nevada. When neighboring states passed laws requiring couples to wait for blood tests in an effort to curb venereal disease, Nevada kept its unrestricted laws. In 1931 Nevada's legislature legalized quick divorces as well as gambling.

Wee Kirk of the Heather wedding chapel on Las Vegas Boulevard, Las Vegas, 1949. The chapel was open for weddings day and night, and all the frills and necessities were available, including the wedding license. Nepwork Photos

Nevada's easy divorce law assured that a divorce could be obtained upon establishing <u>six weeks'</u> <u>residence in the state.</u> Las Vegas received a publicity bonanza when Ria Gable, wife of film super- star Clark Gable, arrived in town in early 1939 to obtain a divorce. Guy McAfee timed the open- ing of his 91-Club to coincide with the publicity surrounding Mrs. Gable's divorce, and down- town clubs announced expansion plans. Taking their cues from Ria Gable, increasing numbers of people chose Las Vegas as a chic place to dissolve their marriages. Several old ranches in the Las Vegas area, including the Kiel Ranch, were converted into dude ranches catering to guests estab- lishing Nevada residency for a divorce. This montage of photos was assembled by the Las Vegas Chamber of Commerce to promote Las Vegas as a divorce capital; it appeared in newspapers throughout the country. Nepwork Photos

Nevada's easy divorce laws were a growing source of revenue throughout the 1930s. When Ria Langham Gable, wife of film star Clark Gable, came to Las Vegas for a divorce in early 1939, she made national headlines. Ria played the role of the happy divorcée in Las Vegas while Clark and Carole Lombard carried out their affair in Los Angeles, enhancing Las Vegas's image as a delightfully sin- ful place. World War II made Las Vegas a sought-after destination for unhappy partners. Between mid-1945 and mid-1946, for example, the state of Nevada granted 20,000 divorces—more than were granted in all of New York, although Nevada had only a fraction of New York's population.

Gambling had flourished in Nevada since its territorial days. In 1911, during the Progressive Era, a nationwide wave of reform resulted in the passage of state laws that closed the casinos. The laws were amended in 1915 following public

EXTRA

LAS VEGAS AGE

GAMBLING BILL PASSES SENATE
ASSEMBLY TO O. K. AMENDMENT

SHIPS SEARCH   MAYOR WALKER
FOR MISSING   SAYS HEALTH
ON ICE FLOE   COMES FIRST

SIX COMPANIES ANNOUNCES
NEW RAILWAY CONSTRUCTION

*Measure Will Become Law As
Soon As Senate Amendment Passes
Assembly and Signed By Governor*

The Gambling Bill, the much disputed measure that will legalize all types of gambling within the state of Nevada, passed the Senate today. The Senate voted an amendment to the measure already passed by the Assembly, placing the control of the measure in the hands of city officials within incorporated cities. A poll of the Assembly assures the passage of the bill with the amendment

An obscure Humboldt County rancher introduced a bill into the Nevada State Legislature in 1931 to legalize gambling in the state, and the bill became law a month later. The legislation proved pivotal to the future of Las Vegas and the entire state of Nevada. Nepwork Photos

outcries. Card games were legalized with some restrictions, and slot machines were reinstated, though without monetary prizes. The antigambling laws that remained were lightly enforced.

The state law that legalized gambling in 1931 gave cities and counties the power to collect taxes and issue gambling licenses. At first the Clark County commissioners issued licenses for slot machines only. The town of Las Vegas passed an ordinance confining gaming establishments to Fremont between First and Third streets. Although the boundary was eventually extended to Fifth Street and beyond, its intent was to keep gambling from spilling over into residential neighborhoods. Table games were soon added in Clark County, and establishments proliferated in downtown Las Vegas and in areas outside the city limits.

In 1931 California gambler Tony Cornero and his brothers constructed the Meadows Club on the outskirts of town, along the Boulder Highway near what is now the intersection of Fremont and Charleston. The Meadows Club was Las Vegas's first real nightclub and cost $31,000 to build. During the 1930s, the three Gumm Sisters—including Frances Gumm, later famous as Judy Garland—appeared there. In 1929 there were no nightclubs located along Highway 91—the Los Angeles highway, later known as the Strip. Beginning in the early 1930s, several small night spots were opened on the Los Angeles highway south of town, including the Pair-O-Dice Club. The new night spots competed with downtown establishments, such as the Apache Club, the Northern Club, and the Golden Camel.

Inside the Northern Club, located on Fremont Street, 1935. The Northern Club was the first estab-lishment issued a gaming license by Clark County officials following legalization of gambling in 1931. The Vegas Club, the Apache Club, the Boulder Club, and the Northern Club constituted the "big four" on Fremont Street in the late 1930s. Here a big game is under way, judging from the crowd that has gathered. Nepwork Photos

*Tony Cornero, pictured seated at far left, was among the first to recognize the opportunities pro-
vided by Nevada's legalization of gambling in 1931. Only months after gambling was legalized,
Cornero and his brothers opened the Meadows Club, a sumptuous casino located just beyond the
Las Vegas city limits on the Boulder Highway. Photo circa 1933, probably at the Meadows.*
University of Nevada, Las Vegas–Dickinson Library Special Collections

*The Meadows Club stood near what is now the intersection of Fremont and Charleston streets.
Photo dated 1931.* University of Nevada, Las Vegas–Dickinson Library Special Collections

A Las Vegas photographer won Life *magazine's picture of the week award for this November 1951 shot of the mushroom cloud from an atomic bomb test.* Las Vegas News Bureau

6

Federal Projects Promote Growth

The construction of Hoover Dam was the first of Las Vegas's opportunities to move beyond its dependence on the railroad and early mining efforts in the area. World War II brought the next federal projects, which allowed Las Vegas to shake off its past. In 1940 the population of the city stood at about 8,000; in the coming decades, Las Vegas's rate of growth would be among the fastest in the nation.

The Birth of Nellis Air Force Base

In 1940 the U.S. Army Air Corps came to Las Vegas to investigate the possibility of using the community airport as a training facility. Western Air Express (which later became Western Airlines) owned the airport; the airline sold it to the city, which in turn signed a lease in January 1941 allowing the Corps to establish a gunnery school at the airport. Nearly 2,000 men were stationed at the airfield that summer, and the population of Las Vegas doubled, thanks to workers, contractors, businesses, and military personnel brought in by or attracted to the base. By 1943 at least 8,000 servicemen were stationed at the airfield; the number grew to 11,000 by the end of World War II. With a captive audience just outside the city's limits, the movie houses, casinos, and bars of Las Vegas did a booming business.

After Germany's surrender, the airfield functioned as a separation center and processing unit for personnel. Chamber of Commerce officials in Las Vegas asked the military to make the airfield a permanent facility; the military agreed but insisted that commercial air traffic be moved to another site. In 1947 a bond issue was passed to build a commercial airport—McCarran Airfield—closer to the city.

Three years later the original airfield was renamed Nellis Air Force Base. The base's 3,000 employees had a payroll of about $8 million, which constituted seven percent of Clark County's income. Base employment doubled in 1951 with the advent of the Korean War.

A Second Boom: Magnesium for the War Effort

A major injection of federal money into Las Vegas occurred when the government signed a contract with Basic Magnesium Incorporated in 1941 to mine and process magnesium needed for bombs during World War II. The magnesium would be mined from a massive deposit at Gabbs, Nevada, 300 miles north of Las Vegas. A location in the Las Vegas Valley halfway between Las Vegas and Boulder City was chosen for the processing plant because of the ready availability of water and power from Hoover Dam.

Work began on the construction of the processing plant—the world's largest—in 1941. By July, nearly 14,000 workers were employed at the construction site. The plant was completed in May 1943 and, once in operation, employed more than 6,000 workers. The plant is said to have supplied 23 percent of the magnesium used in the allied bombing of Europe.

The necessity of housing workers involved in the construction and operation of Basic Magnesium led to the founding of nearby Henderson (named for Charles Henderson, former chairman of the Reconstruction Finance Corporation). The town of Henderson began with four housing developments. Basic Village and Victory Village were for white employees and their families. A third, Carver Park, housed black employees and their families. Single white—and a few black—employees were housed at Anderson Camp near Carver Park, first in tents and later in dormitories. The new town quickly became the third largest in the state, with about 1,000 homes for workers

Working and living conditions were not particularly good at the plant, especially at first, and many workers resigned after a few weeks or months in the desert. The high turnover of workers was a serious concern for management—the nation was at war and labor was in short supply. Judges as far away as Los Angeles helped keep the plant supplied with workers by sentencing vagrants, bums, and outcasts to thirty days in jail or at the Las Vegas construction site.

When Basic Magnesium shut down in 1944, most of the plant's 13,000 employees left Nevada. Enrollment in Henderson's schools fell by two-thirds and over half the houses were vacated; Carver Park and Victory Village were nearly abandoned. In 1948 the state of Nevada assumed ownership of the magnesium plant for $24 million. The plant was next turned over to private industrial interests; by 1951, 2,500 workers were employed there. Henderson grew steadily and, in June 1953, became an incorporated city. The city experienced rapid growth in the 1980s. According to the 1990 census, Henderson's population was 60,408.

Interior of the Basic Magnesium plant under construction, July 1942.
University of Nevada, Las Vegas–Dickinson Library Special Collections

Housing for workers at the Basic Magnesium processing plant, Henderson, Nevada, April 1942.
University of Nevada, Las Vegas–Dickinson Library Special Collections

A severe housing shortage existed while the plant was being constructed. Here a sign points to a "court" in Henderson where cabins and tents could be rented. Las Vegas was still very much a racially segregated community, as the sign indicates. Circa 1942. University of Nevada, Las Vegas–Dickinson Library Special Collections

The Biggest "Boom" of All: The Nevada Test Site

The Nevada Test Site was established sixty miles north of Las Vegas in late 1950 to test atomic weapons. From 1951 to 1958 more than one hundred atomic tests were conducted in the atmosphere above the facility. The flash of light from the blast and the mushroom cloud that followed were usually visible in Las Vegas, and journalists flocked to the town for a firsthand report on the tests. Local officials were surprised by the publicity. For years tourists streamed into town from southern California to witness the tests, which usually took place at dawn and were announced the night before on the radio. One writer wrote, "Las Vegas is finding the government A-bombs bouncing the greatest tourist lure since the invention of the nickel slot machines" (Kaufman, 1974:90). In 1963 all testing moved underground with the signing of the Limited Test Ban Treaty.

Over the years the Nevada Test Site has been the scene of more than nine hundred announced nuclear weapons tests. In the 1980s atomic testing accounted directly and indirectly for about nine percent of southern Nevada's economic activity. A law passed by Congress and signed by President George Bush in 1992 called for the phasing out of testing at the facility during the 1990s. Efforts are now under way to transform the site into a solar-energy (or other type of energy) research and power-generating facility.

Atomic tests usually took place at dawn. In this picture, taken in April 1953, the flash from the blast can be seen on the horizon to the north of Las Vegas behind the tower and buildings at the old El Rancho Vegas, located at what is now Sahara and the Strip. On the lower left of the photo are spectators. Nepwork Photos

When the government first announced that testing of atomic weapons would take place at the Nevada Test Site, local officials were worried that the tests would have a negative effect on Las Vegas's nascent tourism economy, but they went along with the effort for patriotic reasons. As it turned out, the testing was anything but a drag on tourism—it became a tourism bonanza. A number of businesses in town included "atomic" in their name, and atomic cocktails were available at many local bars. This attitude is clearly evident in this publicity photo from the early 1950s. Las Vegas News Bureau

THE LOMBARD PLANE CRASH

Carole Lombard was one of the best loved of Hollywood's performers in the years before World War II. She had a long list of hit films and by 1937 was the highest paid female movie star, earning $465,000 a year. In 1939, after a much-publicized affair, Lombard married Clark Gable, then the most popular actor in America. Less than three years later, on January 16, 1942, Lombard and twenty-one other people died in a plane crash that veteran Las Vegas newspaperman John Cahlan described as the most important news story that ever came out of Las Vegas.

Lombard was a patriotic citizen and was determined to do her part to help her country win World War II, which the United States had just entered. Accompanied by her mother, Bessie Peters, and Gable's personal public relations man, Otto Winkler, she traveled by train to Indianapolis for a war-bond promotion. Lombard's schedule in Indianapolis was hectic, and she dreaded the long train ride back to California. Lombard wanted to fly home, but her companions did not. The decision to take the plane was made by the flip of a coin.

All direct flights were booked, but Lombard found three cancellations on a TWA flight out of New York that would make half a dozen stops before arriving in California. Lombard's mother, a numerologist, opposed taking the flight, warning that the departure date and several other factors were signs of an impending accident or a death. Lombard ignored her mother's warning, and the party left Indianapolis on a DC-3 Skylab.

In Albuquerque, Lombard and her party were asked to yield their seats to members of the Army Air Corps, but Lombard was too close to home to stop.

Carole Lombard and Clark Gable, circa 1939.
Author's photo collection

Although the plane was scheduled for a stop at Boulder City, the pilot, Wayne C. Williams, asked air traffic control in Burbank to reroute the plane through Las Vegas since there were no landing lights at Boulder City.

At 6:36 P.M. the plane landed at Las Vegas's Western Airline terminal (now Nellis Air Force Base), and 225 gallons of fuel were taken on. The plane lifted off at 7:07 P.M., and seven minutes later the plane broke radio contact. At precisely 7:23 P.M., residents of the Las Vegas Valley heard a tremendous explosion. The plane, traveling at more than 150 miles per hour, had slammed into the top of Mount Potosi, just a few miles southwest of Las Vegas. The plane had failed to clear the mountaintop by fewer than 60 feet. The gasoline tank, located under the passengers, had exploded.

Shortly before 8:00 P.M., Gable was notified in Hollywood that Lombard's plane had gone down; his movie studio chartered a plane for him. Gable arrived in Las Vegas at 1:00 A.M. Saturday and

Sadly, Las Vegas made the headlines throughout the country on January 17, 1942, when the wreckage of a TWA plane carrying Carole Lombard and others was found near the summit of Mount Potosi. This headline from the Las Vegas Evening Review Journal *tells of the tragedy.*

rented a bungalow at the El Rancho Vegas, where he awaited news from the search parties. His old friend Spencer Tracy rushed to his side.

On Sunday, search parties sent word that there were no survivors. Lombard's body was identified by her blond hair. A soldier found a damaged diamond and ruby clip that Gable had given Lombard, and friends said Gable carried it in a small box worn around his neck until he remarried years later. Carole Lombard was buried at Forest Lawn Cemetery in Los Angeles on January 22, 1942.

The investigation into the cause of the plane crash was intensive. The FBI entered the matter to determine if the flight could have been sabotaged. Investigators concluded that the probable cause was Captain Williams's failure to adjust his flight chart when landing in Las Vegas instead of Boulder City. The coordinates of the old flight plan would have taken him on a safe path from Boulder City to Burbank, but the same coordinates out of the Las Vegas airport produced tragedy.

El Rancho Vegas showroom dancers, 1949. Las Vegas News Bureau

The Strip Is Born — With Thanks to Los Angeles

Gambling grew in Las Vegas largely as a result of gambling reform in Los Angeles. Illegal prostitution and gambling had flourished openly for many years in Los Angeles, but in 1938 the citizens elected a mayor who promised to target those activities. Los Angeles police began to enforce the laws, driving out a number of operators—who quickly moved to Las Vegas.

Captain Guy McAfee, commander of the Los Angeles police department's vice squad—himself a long-time operator of illegal gambling operations—resigned and moved to Las Vegas in 1938. He purchased the Pair-O-Dice Club, a small nightclub about four miles south of Fremont Street on Highway 91, the Los Angeles Highway. Not long after McAfee's arrival, Clark County's district attorney, Roland Wiley, received a call from Nevada's governor, Edward P. "Ted" Carville. Carville indicated that the state did not like McAfee's presence and suggested that Wiley run him out of town. Wiley pointed out to the governor that McAfee may have engaged in illegal activities in California but had done nothing wrong in Nevada. McAfee and the Pair-O-Dice remained, and other gamblers soon followed.

In a sense Guy McAfee was the father of the modern Las Vegas Strip: It was he who first referred to the four-mile stretch of Highway 91 south of downtown as "the Strip," after Sunset Strip in Los Angeles.

So Much for "Worthless" Property: El Rancho Vegas

California hotel man Thomas Hull was the first individual to really see the potential for the construction of casinos along Highway 91. Hull had been invited by local businessmen to visit Las Vegas. They were certain he would see the town's potential, and he did. Persuaded in part by lower land costs and taxes, Hull chose not to construct a casino downtown but instead set his sights on a property on the highway at the intersection of San Francisco Avenue (now Sahara Avenue). He purchased approximately thirty-three acres from a woman who was glad to get rid of the "worthless" property for $150 per acre (Stamos, 1979a:7).

Hull hired a prestigious Los Angeles architectural firm to design a motor hotel, which featured a ranch-like Spanish mission motif. El Rancho Vegas opened its doors on April 3, 1941, with a gala celebration. Old-timers in town and boosters who had long lamented the absence of a high-class hotel recognized that a new era had begun in Las Vegas.

Convenience was the watchword at El Rancho Vegas, with lodging, parking, restaurants, shops, a travel agency, horseback riding, swimming, and, of course, gambling among the services provided. The casino was small compared to those in Las Vegas today—it had only one craps table, two blackjack tables, and one roulette wheel—but it became the model for future casinos.

El Rancho Vegas also offered entertainment, including a chorus line of scantily clad girls with good figures (plump, by today's standards), brought in from Hollywood. Big names, including Milton Berle, Jackie Gleason, Jimmy Durante, Nat King Cole, and, later, Dean Martin, Jerry Lewis, Peggy Lee, Sammy Davis, Jr., and Andy Williams, were used to attract and hold crowds and high rollers. By 1960 the original motel with 40 cottages had expanded to 69 buildings with 220 rooms.

Construction site of the El Rancho Vegas, late 1940.
Nepwork Photos

Located on the west side of what was to become the Strip, at what is now the inte[r]section of Las Vegas Boulevard and Saha[ra] the El Rancho Vegas opened in 1941 with 63 rooms, most of which were bungalows The sign in front boasted of air condition ing, which had only recently become avai[l] able and was an important factor in the development of Las Vegas. Circa 1945.
University of Nevada, Las Vegas–Dickinson Library
Special Collections

El Rancho Vegas showroom, circa 1945.
Like many of the early resorts in Las Vegas,
the El Rancho Vegas featured a Western
motif, in keeping with the town's frontier
image. The showroom seated 250. Nepwork
Photos

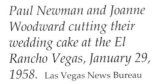

Paul Newman and Joanne
Woodward cutting their
wedding cake at the El
Rancho Vegas, January 29,
1958. Las Vegas News Bureau

Second on the Scene: The (Last) Frontier

The Frontier was the second major resort to be constructed on what was to become the Las Vegas Strip. Originally called the Last Frontier, it was built by R. E. Griffith, whose family owned a chain of 475 movie theaters. Like Hull before him, Griffith, with his nephew William J. (Bill) Moore, decided to build along Highway 91. He chose the site of the old Pair-O-Dice Club, about a mile south of El Rancho Vegas.

The grand opening of the Last Frontier was held October 30, 1942. The complex was a creative study of the Old West: Headboards in the guest rooms looked like large oxen yokes, and cow horns were used throughout the hotel. The main showroom and dining room were decorated with Navajo artwork; a trophy room displayed mounted animals. The mahogany-backed bar came from the old Arizona Club. The hotel, which had 107 rooms, featured a swimming pool that could easily be seen from the highway to tempt hot and dusty travelers.

On the grounds to the north of the main complex, Bill Moore, who was the vice-president and general manager of the Frontier until it was sold in 1951, built Last Frontier Village, a re-creation of a frontier village. The buildings included a rustic chapel known as the Little Church of the West.

Moore sold the Last Frontier in August 1951. The hotel changed owners again in April 1955, and much of the edifice was torn down to make room for a larger facility. The hotel was renamed the New Frontier; the bar in its Cloud Nine Lounge was reputed to be the world's longest.

Guy McAfee, 1954.

University of Nevada, Las Vegas–Dickinson Library Special Collections

The Last Frontier Hotel was constructed on the site that had been occupied by the Pair-O-Dice (pictured above), purchased by Guy McAfee and renamed the 91-Club. R. E. Griffith and McAfee dickered over the price of the Pair-O-Dice. Once the deal was concluded, McAfee, thinking he had gotten the best of Griffith, said mockingly, "If you'd bargained harder, I would've sold it for less." Griffith retorted, "If you'd have bargained harder, I would've paid more." Circa 1940.

University of Nevada, Las Vegas–Dickinson Library Special Collections

Aerial view of the Last Frontier, circa 1944. On the far right between the rodeo grounds and one of the main buildings is the Little Church of the West. Nepwork Photos

Swimming pool and guests, Last Frontier Hotel, circa 1942. Nepwork Photos

Last Frontier stagecoach used to transport V.I.P.s to and from hotel. Circa mid-1940s. Nepwork
Photos

*Actor Ronald Reagan at the Last Frontier Hotel, 1954. Reagan's performance in Las
Vegas was not considered a success, and he was only booked once at the hotel.* Las Vegas News Bureau

Bill Moore, vice-president and general manager of the Last Frontier until it was sold in 1951. Moore was said to have started the hotel's traditional sumptuous Sunday morning buffet breakfast. For years, many Las Vegans would breakfast at the Last Frontier after church. Circa 1950. Nepwork Photos

In 1954, the Little Church of the West was moved from the north end of the Last Frontier to a spot on the south side, where it remained for many years. Later the church was moved to the south end of the Strip, where it now sits next to the Hacienda Hotel. Nepwork Photos

The Flamingo Adds Some Color

True to its name, the Flamingo—the third major resort built on the Strip—had an unusual and colorful beginning. Lucky Luciano, a mobster in New York, was behind the construction of the resort. Old-timers in Las Vegas say the mob was actually encouraged to move into Las Vegas by a small group of local businessmen who did not have the support of the majority of their colleagues.

Ben "Bugsy" Siegel, a former hitman who supervised Luciano's Los Angeles interests, raised over $1 million and in 1945 received the approval of Meyer Lansky, Luciano's financial genius, to construct a luxurious resort in Las Vegas. At first Siegel tried to obtain and expand the El Cortez Hotel located on Fremont Street. City officials were well aware of Siegel's mob connections and refused to give him the water and electric power services he needed for the proposed project. Rebuffed, Siegel looked for a place outside the city limits where the resort could use well water and generate its own power. It was not Siegel, however, who initiated construction of the Flamingo.

Southern California businessman and gambler William Wilkerson, Sr., had begun constructing a hotel and casino in 1945. After spending $600,000 on the hotel, Wilkerson found he was broke, and he put out the word that he needed partners. Wilkerson was soon contacted by Siegel and his partners, who represented themselves as eastern businessmen. Wilkerson sold a two-thirds interest to Siegel at that point; Siegel purchased the remaining third from Wilkerson two weeks before the Flamingo opened.

The Flamingo Hotel construction site, 1945, looking west. The large building in the center of the photo is the Oregon Building; just below Highway 91 is the distinctive Flamingo tower, under construction. Directly across the highway (top third of photo) is the present site of Caesars Palace; to the upper left of the photo is the site of the Dunes. The frame buildings on the left of the Flamingo stand on the present site of the Barbary Coast, with Bally's located across the street.
Nepwork Photos

LAS VEGAS

Front exterior of the Flamingo Hotel, 1947, with the newly added neon flamingo on the top of its sign.
Nepwork Photos

By 1955, the Last Frontier had been expanded and its name changed to the New Frontier. The sign announces that Sammy Davis, Jr., is playing in the showroom and that the Mary Kay Trio, a popular lounge act in Las Vegas for many years, is playing in the Cloud Nine Lounge. Circa 1955.
Nepwork Photos

Grounds of the Flamingo Hotel, not long after it opened on December 26, 1946. The Oregon Building in the background featured luxurious rooms, and the fourth floor tower was the quarters of Bugsy Siegel. The Oregon Building had 77 rooms with 16 fire exits. Some of its staircases led nowhere, and underground passages wound through a maze of steam pipes and boiler rooms before exiting out of doors—all in an effort to foil any attempt on Siegel's life. The closets in his suite featured escape hatches that led down to a garage with a getaway car. Nepwork Photos

The casino of the Flamingo Hotel, circa 1953. Officials at the Flamingo changed the hotel's front tower to suggest champagne bubbles. In the casino the bubble motif appeared on the ceiling. Comedian Joe E. Lewis is playing in the showroom when this photo was taken—the showroom has Lewis's slogan, "Post Time," at its entrance. Nepwork Photos

Gus Greenbaum (left) and Moe Sedway, mob figures active in Las Vegas for a number of years. In 1947, Greenbaum, Sedway, and Morris Rosen took control of the Flamingo.

University of Nevada, Las Vegas–Dickinson Library Special Collections

The sprawling facility was constructed on barren desert about one mile south of the Last Frontier, on the Los Angeles highway. The hotel featured 150 luxurious rooms, a health club and gymnasium, steam rooms, tennis courts, badminton facilities, squash and handball courts, a huge swimming pool, a trap-shooting range, a nine-hole golf course, stables with forty high-quality saddle horses, and a variety of shops. Siegel insisted on expensive, imported furnishings; bathrooms had individual sewer lines.

A shortage of building materials and cost overruns caused by Siegel's perfectionism—and perhaps, graft—quickly resulted in costs that ballooned from $1 million to $6 million. Siegel scraped funds together, and the mob reluctantly kicked in additional money. Because the mob was anxious to see a return on its investment, the grand opening was held December 26, 1946, with only the casino, restaurant, and theater open to the public.

The opening was a big flop despite the presence of top entertainers such as Georgie Jessel and Jimmy Durante. The celebrities and high rollers necessary to produce a big take at the gaming tables didn't show. The three-story waterfall in front of the hotel was to splash down on opening night, but Siegel, ever superstitious, refused to have the water turned on when it was discovered that a cat had crawled into the bottom of the pool that day and had given birth to a litter of kittens. To remove them would have been "hard luck" (Stamos, 1979b:8). A dress code requiring coat and tie kept average gamblers away; the code was quickly abolished by a local advertising agency hired by Siegel to improve the resort's publicity. A campaign in Los Angeles with posters on streetcars reading "Everybody Welcome" soon produced the desired crowds.

The Flamingo's formal opening in March 1947 was successful, but the mob had become disillusioned with Siegel, supposedly not just because he had been too extravagant. Some think the mob discovered that Siegel's girlfriend, Virginia Hill, had been depositing large sums of money in Swiss bank accounts and shopping for houses in Zurich. On June 20, 1947, Siegel was gunned down in his mansion in Beverly Hills.

Old-timers in Las Vegas claim that the setup was more elaborate. The mob had wanted to do away with Siegel for some time, but his security was too tight, and they dared not outrage officials in Nevada by killing him there. Virginia Hill had been an attractive hooker in Florida, and old-timers say she was sent to Las Vegas by the mob to seduce Siegel and lure him out of town so that he could be safely killed. Minutes before Siegel was shot in Los Angeles, three men, Gus Greenbaum, Morris Rosen, and Moe Sedway—all members of the mob—walked into the general offices of the Flamingo and took control.

The Thunderbird

The Thunderbird—the fourth major hotel on the Strip—opened in 1948. The Old West provided the theme for the hotel's design. Charges that mob figures held an interest in the hotel resulted in the loss of its license in 1955, and although it was reopened, its image was damaged.

The Thunderbird was purchased in 1964 by the Del Webb Corporation for $9.5 million; in 1972 it was sold to Caesars Palace. The owner of the Dunes, Major Arteburn Riddle, purchased the property in 1977, enlarged the hotel, and changed its name to the Silverbird. In 1981 the hotel was purchased by Ed Torres and renamed the El Rancho. The original El Rancho Vegas had been located across the street—the two facilities had no connection.

The Thunderbird was the first Las Vegas hotel to promote itself as a convention facility. After its bookings slowed, it was closed for an extended period in 1991.

The Golden Nugget Outshines the Rest

In 1945 Guy McAfee opened the Golden Nugget with associates Roscoe Thomas and Art Ham, Sr. The Golden Nugget, which stands at the corner of Second and Fremont, was designed in a San Francisco–Barbary Coast style. At the time it was built, it had the largest casino in Las Vegas, known as the Million Dollar Casino. Three years later McAfee added an electric sign 100 feet high that billed the Nugget as "the brightest night spot in the world" (Moehring, 1989:50–51). Fremont Street became known as Glitter Gulch, as other operators on the street either remodeled or rebuilt to keep up with their new upscale competitor.

Interior of the Golden Nugget, circa 1946. Nepwork Photos

Fremont Street, looking west, 1948. The Golden Nugget was at this time Las Vegas's largest casino. The electric sign had recently been added. Note the banner stretching across Fremont Street welcoming President Harry Truman, vice-presidential candidate Alvin Barkley, and longtime Nevada Congressman Walter Baring. Nepwork Photos

The Campaign That Made the Desert Bloom

Las Vegas's transformation into a tourist center during the late 1940s owes much to the efforts of Maxwell Kelch, who became president of the Chamber of Commerce in 1944. The owner of KENO, Las Vegas's only radio station at the time, Kelch understood the power of advertising.

Under his direction Chamber officials came to view Las Vegas as a business; to survive and grow, the business had to advertise. Chamber officials studied how Palm Springs, Miami Beach, and Tucson, Arizona, had promoted themselves as centers of tourism. In 1945 the Chamber invited eight advertising and publicity agencies to present proposals for promoting Las Vegas. The contract was awarded to J. Walter

Maxwell Kelch, pictured in 1953 with a planning map showing the growth along the Strip from 1943 to 1953. Nepwork Photos

One of the best aerial photos of the Strip taken during the early 1950s. In this view looking north, the Flamingo is visible in the foreground, and farther along the Strip the Sands Hotel is under construction. The Last Frontier is visible on the left, and the El Rancho Vegas can be seen farther north. Photo taken in 1952. Nepwork Photos

Thompson Company, one of the premier advertising agencies in the world. In the campaign that followed, Las Vegas was promoted as a place with a beautiful climate and location, amid scenic sites. Ads focused on luxurious hotels that provided top entertainment in a western city representing the "last frontier." Southern California was the first target of the campaign.

As a result of the publicity, magazine and newspaper writers began to arrive in Las Vegas in search of stories. Even potentially adverse publicity (such as the

LAS VEGAS

nearby detonation of A-bombs) and "hatchet jobs" focusing on gambling, divorce, and mob influence failed to hurt the city's emerging image. These stories only increased the desire of millions to visit the city that was naughty but nice. Soon the image of Las Vegas as an adventurous place free of conventional moralism was firmly established. The town was poised for the dramatic growth that was to follow in the 1950s.

From its earliest days as an entertainment mecca, Las Vegas has been known for its many beautiful women, many of whom danced in the chorus lines in the shows on the Strip. In 1976 Mario Puzo, author of The Godfather, *wrote in his book* Inside Las Vegas, *"Las Vegas has more beautiful women than any town its size in the world. It may have as many beautiful women as any city in the world no matter what its size" (p. 176). Pictured here are women in the chorus lines at the Frontier, circa 1945, and the Flamingo and Thunderbird, circa 1950.* Las Vegas News Bureau

Everybody has heard of a "floating craps game." The idea of setting a craps table in the pool of the Sands, along with a twenty-one table and slot machines, was, in the summer of 1953, one of the most successful publicity stunts ever to come out of Las Vegas. Photos of gamblers in the pool at the Sands ran in nearly every major newspaper in the United States. Las Vegas News Bureau

CHAPTER 8

A Decade of Development: The 1950s

Maxwell Kelch's publicity campaign combined with the growing popularity of the automobile, postwar national prosperity, and a population boom in southern California to produce a jump in tourism in Las Vegas. It was clear to city officials and developers that more facilities were needed.

The developers responded with a number of new hotels constructed downtown and along Highway 91, the Strip. Initial development along the Strip followed the pattern, modest by today's standards, that was pioneered by the El Rancho Vegas—bungalow-style rooms adjoining or connecting to a casino, restaurant, and lounge. The hotels gradually became larger and more sophisticated, eventually resulting in the giant, self-contained, extremely profitable resort hotels now found on the Strip.

The Desert Inn Sets the Pace

Considered Las Vegas's classiest hotel for a generation following its construction, the Desert Inn was the dream of Wilbur Clark, a former bellman and California bar owner who had joined the migration of gamblers to Las Vegas following the election in 1938 of Los Angeles reform-minded mayor Fletcher Bowlon. Clark purchased a share of the El Rancho Vegas in 1944 and then built the Players Club, a small operation on Highway 91, and the Monte Carlo Club, located downtown. A year later he bought land directly across from the Last Frontier and, after selling his interest in the El Rancho Vegas in 1946, began construction of the Desert Inn, named after the Desert Inn Hotel in Palm Springs, which he admired.

Clark did not have the finances to complete construction, and the facility sat vacant during 1947 and 1948. Construction resumed in 1949 after he received additional financing from investors from Detroit and Cleveland who had mob ties and previous experience with illegal gambling in several states.

The hotel opened to rave reviews on April 24, 1950. Reporters from major newspapers and magazines across the nation were flown in at the hotel's expense to cover the opening, which included performances by Edgar Bergen and Charlie McCarthy. The first week's profits totaled $750,000, including $90,000 from the bar. During the first year of operation the monthly gross income for the casino was $250,000; net profit for the first year was just under $2 million.

Spread over the inn's 17 acres were 300 rooms styled in Old West decor and equipped with individual thermostats—an innovation at the time. Room prices began at $5. The casino, at 2,400 square feet, was then Nevada's largest. It featured five craps tables, three roulette wheels, four blackjack games, and seventy-five slot machines, and employed sixty people.

Wilbur Clark, 1950.
Nepwork Photos

Interior of the casino at the Desert Inn on opening day, April 24, 1950. This photo appeared in a popular magazine in a story about the Desert Inn's opening. The Desert Inn was considered the classiest resort in Las Vegas at the time.
Nepwork Photos

Exterior of the Desert Inn when it opened in 1950. Nepwork Photos

Club Bingo in 1948, about four years before it was remodeled, expanded, and renamed the Sahara. Nepwork Photos

The Sahara Hotel, 1952. Las Vegas News Bureau

In Quick Succession: The Sahara and the Sands

The Sahara began operation in 1947 as the modest Club Bingo, a 300-seat bingo parlor at the corner of San Francisco Street (now Sahara) and the Strip. The success of Club Bingo led its owner, Milton Prell, to expand and remodel it with an unusual African decor. The club's name was changed to the Sahara Hotel; it featured the Congo Room, Casbar Lounge, and Caravan Room restaurant, in keeping with the African theme.

The Sahara opened October 7, 1952; Ray Bolger was the featured entertainer. The Sahara was expanded in 1953 and again in 1966, when a 14-story, 200-room tower was built; it was the tallest structure in the state at the time.

The Sands Hotel, December 1952. Nepwork Photos

In 1964 the Sahara Hotel sponsored two performances by the Beatles, in what was possibly the largest single entertainment event in Las Vegas history, surpassing even Elvis Presley's appearances. More than 8,400 frenzied fans jammed into the convention center, which had a maximum seating capacity of 7,000, for each of the performances.

The Sands was opened on December 15, 1952—less than three months after the Sahara. It was built by Jake Friedman, who had come to Las Vegas from Houston, Texas, with a plan to build a luxury hotel. He purchased the LaRue Restaurant on Highway 91 and began constructing his hotel in early 1952.

While visiting the construction site one day, Friedman was asked to give a working name to the structure, which he had planned to call the Holiday Inn after the popular movie starring Bing Crosby and Danny Kaye. He replied, "There's so much sand in this damned place that my socks are full of it! So why don't we call it 'The Sand' until it's finished." "But Mr. Friedman," responded the builder, "You can't just say 'The Sand.' You must use the plural, 'Sands'." The hotel's name was the Sands from that moment on (Stamos, 1979c:6).

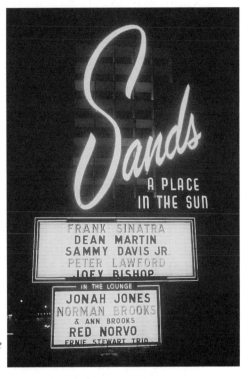

The western edition of Jack Entratter's Copa Girls was featured at the Sands. A Copa Girl had to be tall, leggy, and beautiful; the Copa was considered the highest-status job for a showgirl in Las Vegas at that time. Circa 1955. University of Nevada, Las Vegas–Dickinson Library Special Collections

Frank Sinatra was a regular performer at the Sands during the 1950s. Sinatra's friends, dubbed the "Rat Pack," included Dean Martin, Sammy Davis, Jr., Peter Lawford, and Joey Bishop, whose names are seen on the marquee in this photo from the late 1950s. Their presence lent glamour and prestige to the establishment and to Las Vegas. Nepwork Photos

The Sands cost $5.5 million to construct and was built in a record nine months and four days. Danny Thomas, Billy Eckstine, and Jane Powell were featured at the opening. The Sands originally had 200 rooms located in five 2-story buildings named after famous American racetracks. The buildings were arranged in a semicircle around a half-moon-shaped pool. The Copa—the main showroom—featured the Copa Girls, "the most beautiful girls in the world," to quote the resort's own promotion. The Copa Girls enjoyed high status and were considered to be among the classiest women in Las Vegas. They were for many years the envy of other dancers in town.

Jack Entratter, one of Friedman's partners, had formerly been with the Copacabana in New York, and he had vast connections among celebrities. He helped to establish the Las Vegas tradition of providing top entertainment for hotel guests. During the late 1950s and early 1960s the "Rat Pack" (Frank Sinatra, Dean Martin, Joey Bishop, Sammy Davis, Jr., and Peter Lawford) frequented the Sands. In 1960, while on location for the film *Ocean's 11*, the actors would film during the day and party in the Sands' showroom and lounge until late at night.

In the spring of 1955 actress Grace Kelly and actor Cary Grant, in the white jacket in the background, were at the Sahara. The two starred in the 1955 classic Hitchcock film To Catch a Thief.

Las Vegas News Bureau

Doris Day, Frank Sinatra, and Lauren Bacall at the Sands, 1955.

Las Vegas News Bureau

Dean Martin and Jerry Lewis at a blackjack table, Sands Hotel, 1953.

Las Vegas News Bureau

The Showboat on opening day, September 3, 1954. The hotel resembles a 1840s Mississippi paddle wheeler.

Las Vegas News Bureau

Next on the Scene: The Showboat

The Showboat was the first resort hotel to be constructed someplace other than downtown or along the Strip. Surveys done in early 1954 indicated that the new hub of Las Vegas would be located south of downtown. Persuaded by the surveys, William J. Moore (formerly of the Last Frontier) and a group of investors decided to construct a resort about two miles south of downtown on the highway to Hoover Dam.

The Showboat opened on September 3, 1954. The building was constructed to resemble an 1840s Mississippi paddle wheeler, and its decor was inspired by a Mark Twain novel. It was billed as Las Vegas's first resort hotel, which was technically true since the El Rancho Vegas, Last Frontier, Flamingo, and Desert Inn were located outside of the Las Vegas city limits.

The Showboat, whose prow extended into the swimming pool, was quite an attention-getter; it featured 100 rooms and an 18,000-square-foot casino. The casino was constructed by and initially operated by the Desert Inn. A 500-seat bingo room doubled as a showroom in the evenings.

Because of its location, the Showboat was forced to adopt aggressive marketing techniques to compete with hotels located downtown and on the Strip. It was one of the first hotels, if not the first, to sponsor bus tours from southern California and Phoenix. High rollers were brought in from places as far away as Chicago. The Showboat also became known for its 24-lane bowling alley, which opened in 1959.

The Riviera opened on April 21, 1955, and was the first high-rise hotel on the Strip. It was also one of the first Las Vegas hotels to use elevators. Las Vegas News Bureau

Standing Tall: The Riviera

Opened on April 21, 1955, the Riviera cost $8.5 million to build, and it earned honors as the first high-rise on the Strip. A few skeptics claimed the porous desert floor would not support the weight of the hotel's 9-story tower; so far the fears have been unwarranted. The Riviera was one of the first Las Vegas hotels to use elevators. The hotel contained 250 rooms that emulated European splendor. Its 10,000-square-foot showroom, the Clover Room, was the largest on the Strip for a while.

The Riviera's Miami investors had much to learn about gaming; they filed for bankruptcy three months after the resort opened. Gus Greenbaum, formerly of the Flamingo (and with connections to the mob), was brought in to save the operation. He stayed with the hotel until 1958, when illness forced him to return to his home in Phoenix. On December 3, 1958, Greenbaum and his wife were found dead in their Phoenix bedroom. The murders were never solved.

Following a series of ownership changes during the 1960s, the Riviera was purchased by New York multimillionaire Meshulam Riklis and a group of investors in the 1970s.

Upping the Ante: The Fremont

The Fremont was downtown's response to the Strip's Riviera. Rising 15 stories above the intersection of Fremont and Second streets, it opened on May 18, 1956. The hotel had 155 rooms and cost $6 million to construct and furnish. For several years it was the tallest building in the state, and it sparkled in the sun owing to the quartz chips in its exterior surface. The man behind the Fremont was Ed Levinson, a former newspaper peddler from Chicago who had been a gamer in Kentucky and had also enjoyed success running hotels in Miami.

The Fremont had the reputation of having the finest food in Las Vegas, and it was the first downtown hotel to attract big-name performers. Its Carnival Lounge featured the Jo Ann Jordan Trio, a popular local group, and Jerry and Wayne Newton and the Jets. It was here that Wayne Newton got his start as a performer. He was a teenager at the time and had to be escorted through the casino. Between sets he hung out at the drugstore across the street. Lou Rawls and Kay Starr also performed at the lounge at the beginning of their careers.

During the 1950s the roof of the Fremont was a favored place to view atomic weapons tests from the nearby Nevada Test Site. The blasts and subsequent mushroom clouds were easily seen from that vantage point.

The Fremont, located on Second and Fremont streets downtown, opened May 18, 1956, and, at 15 stories, was the tallest building in the state. The Fremont helped establish Las Vegas's reputation for fine food and popular lounge acts. Nepwork Photos

When the Tropicana opened at the far south end of the Strip in April 1957, it was, at $15 million, the most expensive development in Las Vegas up to that time. The intersection of the Strip and Tropicana Avenue, pictured here just prior to the Tropicana's opening, is now Las Vegas's most active corner, with the Excalibur occupying the corner to the far right, the MGM on the corner to the left of the Tropicana, and New York-New York at lower center. Las Vegas News Bureau

Luxury First: The Tropicana

The Tropicana was the creation of Ben Jaffe, who headed the Fontainebleau Hotel in Miami Beach. Jaffe owned an insurance company and is said to have been involved in punchboard gambling in Mexico. In 1955 he purchased a 40-acre plot of land at the southeast corner of the Strip and Bond Road, now Tropicana Avenue. The Tropicana was designed with a Caribbean theme, reminiscent of Old Havana. It was constructed as a luxury hotel first and a gaming establishment second. Rooms could be reached without going through the casino, violating a cardinal rule of casino design in the 1950s. The hotel's air-conditioning system was powerful enough to cool one thousand homes in Death Valley in the summer; the building was said to contain enough concrete for a 40-mile-long freeway. For years the 60-foot-high fountain that stood in front of the hotel was a landmark on the Strip.

The Tropicana opened on April 4, 1957, with Nevada Lieutenant Governor Rex Bell doing the honors at the ribbon-cutting ceremony. As an indication of the hotel's upscale ambience, Bell was later denied entry to one of its restaurants because he was not wearing a tie. Eddie Fisher starred at the opening. Room rates ranged from $12 to $50 a day.

Backstage view of the Folies Bergère, Tropicana Hotel, circa 1965. Beautiful costuming, music, and choreography—not to mention the showgirls—combine to produce a stunning visual effect. Las Vegas News Bureau

Another high roller tries his luck at the craps table at the Tropicana in the early 1960s. The gamer in the hat was J. Fred Muggs, a well-known television performer.
Nepwork Photos

Two months after the Tropicana's opening, mobster Frank Costello was assassinated in New York. A slip of paper in his pocket is said to have had the figure $651,284 on it, which coincided with the figure for the Tropicana's first twenty-four days of revenues. Observers believed that Phil Kastel, an associate of Jaffe's, was the link between the Tropicana and the mob. Kastel had been chosen to operate the casino but had never been approved by state gaming authorities because of his alleged mob ties. The cloud of suspicion was erased when J. Kell Houssels, longtime Las Vegas businessman and part owner of El Cortez and the Showboat, was brought in to manage the hotel.

Lou Walters, entertainment director for the hotel (and the father of journalist Barbara Walters), was instrumental in bringing the Folies Bergère from Paris in 1959. The show has remained a top attraction in Las Vegas, having thrilled audiences at the hotel for more than three decades.

The S.S. Rex, *named after Tony Cornero's gambling ship anchored off the California coast, circa* 1947. Nepwork Photos

The Stardust's sign, pictured here in one of the first exterior shots of the resort. The sign required 32,000 feet of wiring, 7,100 feet of neon tubing, and 11,000 lamps. It could be seen for over three miles and took more than 84 gallons of automobile paint to cover. The Stardust was the first of the resorts in Las Vegas to feature imported French shows, in this case the Lido de Paris. Circa 1958. Las Vegas News Bureau

Girls from the Lido de Paris show, just off the plane from Paris, trying their first American hot dogs with champagne, 1958. Nepwork Photos

Stardust: The Biggest of Them All

The Stardust was the inspiration of Anthony Stralla, better known as Tony Cornero. He and his brothers came to Las Vegas in 1931 and operated the Meadows Club for several years. From the late 1930s, Cornero operated a gambling ship, the S.S. *Rex*, off the coast of Los Angeles, until state and federal authorities shut the boat down prior to World War II. He then returned to Las Vegas and opened the S.S. Rex Club on the first floor of the Apache Hotel and remained there during the war years.

In 1954 Cornero paid $650,000 for thirty-two acres on the Strip. Working out of his briefcase and not bothering to register with the Securities and Exchange Commission, Cornero sold $4 million of stock for the construction of the Stardust, which was to be the world's largest resort. The hotel was three-fourths complete when Cornero died suddenly of a heart attack while shooting craps at the Desert Inn in mid-1955. Unsubstantiated rumors that Cornero was injected with a drug while in the restroom the night he died, causing his collapse in the casino, still persist. John Factor, brother to cosmetics giant Max Factor, came to the Stardust's rescue. Enchanted with the prospect of owning such a stellar property, Factor and his wife, Rella, put in $10 million to complete it. Factor, who was known in some circles as "Jake the Barber," was reputed to have mob connections.

When the Stardust opened on July 2, 1958, it had 1,000 rooms and was said to be the largest hotel in the world. The hotel's sign reached 27 feet high and stretched 216 feet along the entire front of the resort; it could be seen for more than three miles.

The showroom stage was larger than a basketball court and had six hydraulic lifts that could drop 30 feet below street level or rise 10 feet above the stage. A swimming tank and an ice rink were stored underneath the seats and were rolled out when needed.

The Stardust's Lido de Paris opened with the resort and was the first of the imported French shows to appear on the Strip. The show featured a promenade of European beauties and a fireworks display from the top of a replica of the Eiffel Tower. Before a girl could become a member of the line she had to meet three requirements: She had to have extensive ballet training, stand a minimum height of 5 feet, 8 inches—with most of that as legs—and radiate beauty. The Starlight lounge was the most popular in Las Vegas in the late 1950s and gave a boost to many entertainers.

Dancers from the Lido de Paris, Stardust Hotel, circa 1975. Las Vegas News Bureau

A Convention Center Comes to Town

As the number of hotel rooms in Las Vegas grew during the early 1950s, city leaders began to focus their attention on a new market: conventions. By bringing in large groups of people for business purposes, hotel operators could increase bookings during the traditionally slow part of the week, Sunday through Thursday. Moreover, they could fill the slack periods during the summer months and Christmas season. City boosters envisioned a meeting complex that would attract large exhibits and enable Las Vegas to vie with major convention cities such as New York, Chicago, and Atlantic City.

There was considerable support for the idea for a convention facility, but questions arose as to who would pay for it. In 1955 the Nevada legislature and the Clark County commissioners created the Fair and Recreation Board, which later evolved into the Las Vegas Convention and Visitors Authority (LVCVA). The organization was funded by a room tax levied on all hotel and motel rooms in Clark County.

Las Vegas Convention Center marquee, with the convention center in the background, circa 1980.   Las Vegas News Bureau

The distinctive domed roof of the Convention Center, under construction on Paradise Road, late 1958, looking west. The Riviera Hotel is visible in the background.   Nepwork Photos

In January 1955 a committee was appointed to select a permanent site for a convention facility. Voters approved a bond measure, and in the spring of 1957 construction began on a site east of the Thunderbird Hotel (now El Rancho). The facility opened two years later and cost more than $5 million to build; it featured a 90,000-square-foot hall and parking for 1,800 cars.

Business thrived in the following years. By the 1970s, Las Vegas had become one of the nation's major convention communities.

Aerial view of the Las Vegas Strip, 1955. The recently opened Dunes Hotel can be seen in the foreground. Also evident are the Flamingo, the Frontier, and the Riviera. Note the large amount of vacant land in the vicinity of the Strip at this time. Nepwork Photos

Tropicana showroom, December 1959. In accordance with the norms of the time, audience members are swankily dressed. Nepwork Photos

Liberace and Elvis Presley in Las Vegas, November 1956. Elvis was not appearing; he was in the audience for Liberace's show. Nepwork Photos

In this unusual photo of the Las Vegas Strip, looking north in 1969, a telephoto lens collapses the perspective from the Sands Hotel (where Jerry Lewis was performing) to the Sahara Hotel. Las Vegas News Bureau

Corporate Investment: The 1960s and 1970s

Until the 1960s most reputable banks and investors did not view Nevada resort hotels that featured gambling as legitimate business investments. As a result, resort construction was sometimes financed, directly or indirectly, by figures associated with underworld crime. Not surprisingly, these investors or owners usually had experience in the gambling business.

Despite the sweeping changes enacted by the state of Nevada in 1947 requiring state licensing of all gaming and race-book operations, organized crime continued to be a presence in Las Vegas. U.S. Senator Estes Kefauver and a congressional committee investigated the mob's dealings in Nevada, and in 1955 state politicians responded by creating the Gaming Control Board to investigate and enforce regulations. Control was further strengthened in 1959, and in 1960 the so-called "black book" was created. The book listed the names of those persons who were physically banned from all casinos in the state. Casinos that violated the ban were subject to immediate revocation of their licenses.

Until 1969, the state had required that all stockholders in a gambling business in Nevada be licensed. In 1969 a new law was passed requiring that only major stockholders be licensed. This law made it possible for major American corporations to become active in Las Vegas. Enactment of the law marked a new era in Las Vegas's development and image.

Howard Hughes's purchase in the 1960s of several major hotel properties had the effect of rapidly legitimizing investment in Las Vegas. The eventual presence of companies like Hyatt, Hilton, Ramada, Holiday Inn, MGM, and Bally's not only made vast capital resources available in Las Vegas but ushered in a new era of legitimacy.

Actress Jean Peters and Howard Hughes were married in Tonopah, Nevada, in 1957. Photo circa 1955.
Author's photo collection

Howard Hughes at about age 45, circa 1960. Paul Laxalt, former Nevada governor and a U.S. senator, said, "If Nevada ever had a friend, a real friend, it was Howard Hughes." Hughes's move to Las Vegas in 1966 and subsequent purchase of the Desert Inn, Sands, Frontier, and several smaller gaming properties was one of the most significant events in Las Vegas's history. Author's photo collection

Howard Hughes Lands in Las Vegas

Howard Hughes, one of the most successful and enigmatic businessmen in American history, had a long association with the city of Las Vegas. During the 1940s and 1950s he was a frequent visitor to the city. He enjoyed the city's glamour and in the evenings would go from one casino to another much as an interested observer. He saw potential for the city, predicting it would someday have a population in excess of one million. He thought that the Las Vegas Valley would eventually be the site of an airport for Los Angeles and that supertrains would speed passengers between the two cities.

Hughes had inherited the Hughes Tool Company, which produced oil-well drill bits, from his father. Using the company as a base, he assembled one of the largest fortunes in history. He was an aviation pioneer and test pilot before purchasing RKO Pictures and producing films for several years.

In 1957 Hughes married actress Jean Peters in a ceremony in Tonopah, Nevada. By this time Hughes's eccentricities were well known and he was becoming more and more of a recluse. Although he and Peters were married for fourteen years, they were in each other's company only occasionally.

In 1966 Hughes moved to Las Vegas and ensconced himself on the ninth floor of the Desert Inn. When the management complained that he and his staff were tying up rooms usually made available for high rollers, he bought the hotel. One veteran Las Vegas publicist said, "I think Howard Hughes is the biggest thing that's happened to Las Vegas since, I'd say, Bugsy Siegel" (Demaris, 1969:73).

On his application to the Nevada Gaming Commission, Hughes listed his height, weight, and eye and hair color, but for most of the rest of the requested information he wrote "not available." After purchasing the Desert Inn he went on to acquire the Sands, the Frontier, the Castaways, the Silver Slipper, and the Landmark.

Hughes is said to have chosen Las Vegas because he believed it was one of the last frontiers and one of the last opportunities to build a model city in a place with sufficient undeveloped land and available water. Inspired by this vision, Hughes started adding Las Vegas land to his portfolio in the 1950s. By the late 1960s he had purchased nearly every vacant lot along the Strip in a 3-mile stretch from the Tropicana to the Sahara.

The Las Vegas Strip, looking northeast, circa 1965. The Flamingo Hotel, with its new tower, is in the foreground; the Desert Villa Motel, where the Barbary Coast presently sits, can be seen at the bottom right. On the north side of the Flamingo is the Flamingo Capri Motel, the present location of the Imperial Palace. The Sahara Hotel is visible in the distance, as is the tower of the Landmark Hotel and the dome of the Convention Center. Across the street from the Flamingo, construction is beginning on Caesars Palace. Nepwork Photos

Caesars Palace under construction, 1966. The Flamingo Hotel's champagne tower is visible at the lower right. This shot is especially interesting for the view it gives of the desert to the west of Caesars Palace, an area that is now nearly filled with homes and businesses. Las Vegas News Bureau

Sarno's Magnificent Creations:
Caesars Palace and Circus Circus

Jay Sarno, a successful designer, builder, operator of hotels, and owner of the Cabana motor hotels, saw a need in Las Vegas for a luxury hotel that would buck the trend of Old West architecture and interior design. With financing arranged in 1961 and 1962 through the Teamsters Pension Fund, Sarno planned a lavish hotel, tentatively named the Desert Palace, for the northwest corner of the Strip and Flamingo.

With construction costs of $19 million, Sarno's hotel was suitable in price and design for an emperor. Indeed, the hotel's Greco-Roman motif led Sarno to rename his hotel, Caesars Palace. The hotel featured several innovations, including "Sarno block," cement blocks cut in a latticework design and used in the facade to lower internal temperatures. Eighteen fountains were built along the 135-foot entrance driveway, which was flanked with imported Italian cypress and Florentine statuary. Gold leaf and Brazilian rosewood were used throughout the lobby. Sarno's long experience in the hotel business had convinced him that oval shapes were conducive to relaxation, so the hotel contains many ovals, including an oval-shaped casino.

Caesars Palace opened on August 5, 1966, with the most extravagant dedication Las Vegas had experienced. The price tag for the opening celebration is said to have been in excess of $1 million. The guest list numbered 1,800. Two tons of filet mignon, 300 pounds of crab, 30,000 fresh eggs, 50,000 glasses of champagne, and the largest order of Ukrainian caviar ever placed by a private organization were served. Andy Williams provided entertainment.

When it opened, the 34-acre property included a 14-story tower with 680 rooms and a Circus Maximus theater that seated 800. The hotel featured 25,000 square feet of meeting and exhibition space. The food served in its restaurants was unsurpassed. The management of Caesars Palace made an effort to attract conventions and had bookings worth $42 million before the hotel opened.

In 1969 Caesars Palace was sold to Clifford Perlman, owner and operator of the Lum's restaurant chain, for $60 million. He began a campaign to promote the resort through television, movies, and sporting events such as boxing.

Sarno's next brainchild was Circus Circus, which opened a scant two years

Former world heavyweight boxing champion Joe Louis was a host at Caesars Palace for many years. Louis is pictured here with Johnny Weismuller, best remembered as Tarzan in the movies, circa 1967. Las Vegas News Bureau

Heavyweights Muhammad Ali and Larry Holmes at Caesars Palace, October 2, 1980. Holmes won by TKO Nepwork Photos

Exterior of Caesars Palace, late 1970s.   Las Vegas News Bureau

after Caesars Palace. Circus Circus had no hotel rooms when it opened for business but could claim Las Vegas's only genuine circus arena, complete with a distinctive pink-and-white Big Top, a carnival midway, restaurants, and various other shops and services. *The Guinness Book of World Records* cites Circus Circus as the largest permanent circus in the world.

In accordance with Sarno's plan, trapeze artists, acrobats, jugglers, and magicians entertain spectators daily in the Big Top. A mezzanine, which circles the area where the circus acts perform, is ringed by a midway with live carnival games and a large arcade. Gambling takes place only on the ground level; even so, at 110,000 square feet, the gaming area is among the largest in the industry.

A 400-room hotel tower was completed a few years later, and a subsequent addition brought the total number of rooms to 2,800. In 1974 Nevada gaming executives William G. Bennett and William N. Pennington assumed control of Sarno's corporation and guided it during an innovative, high growth period.

Circus Circus is widely acknowledged to be among the most effectively managed establishments in the gaming resort business. The resort focuses on middle-income patrons and emphasizes providing a good time to a large number of people. This strategy contrasts with that of earlier decades, when Las Vegas resorts catered to a small clientele, especially high rollers.

The Circus Circus complex, circa 1980.
Las Vegas News Bureau

The interior of Circus Circus, December 1968, two months after the casino opened. Here, patrons play blackjack while trapeze artists fly through the air in the back-ground.   Nepwork Photos

Kirk Kerkorian, pictured during the construction of the International Hotel (now the Las Vegas Hilton), October 1968. Nepwork Photos

The Las Vegas Hilton, as seen from the Landmark tower, November 1977. Las Vegas News Bureau

Kirk Kerkorian Flies into Town

Son of Armenian farmers from Fresno, California, Kirk Kerkorian was a crop duster and a flight instructor for the U.S. Army Air Corps before he began flying gamblers between Hawthorne, California, and Las Vegas in a twin-engine Cessna.

By the 1960s Kerkorian had a fleet of jets assembled under the name Trans International Airlines. He sold the airline for $104 million in 1968 and with part of the money purchased major interests in Western Airlines and MGM Studios in Hollywood. A year before the sale Kerkorian purchased a 64.5-acre site located east of the Strip on Paradise Road and began construction of a hotel. In August 1967 he purchased the Flamingo, which he used as a training ground for employees while his huge new hotel was under construction.

The International opened on July 2, 1969, having cost an unheard-of $60 million to complete. It had 24 floors and was the world's largest resort hotel at the time, with 8½ acres covered under one roof. The casino, also then the largest in the world, was 30,000 square feet. It featured white marble and ornate Czechoslovakian chandeliers. The International offered a fittingly international assortment of restaurants—Italian, German, Mexican, and Japanese cuisines could be had at Kerkorian's marbled marvel.

Leading Nevada politicians, including the governor and the state's two senators, were present at the opening along with celebrities such as Lucille Ball, Cary Grant, Phyllis Diller, George Raft, Nancy Sinatra, and Natalie Wood. Entertainment was provided by Barbra Streisand, and Elvis Presley followed two weeks later. In the seven and one-half years that Presley would play the hotel, he never failed to pack its 2,000-seat showroom.

In July 1970 Kerkorian sold the Flamingo and the International to the Hilton Hotel chain. The two resorts have for years accounted for 50 percent or more of the corporation's profits. Kerkorian predicted that the International would lead to the development of another Strip along Paradise Road, but that has not happened—at least not yet.

Kerkorian's (MGM) Grand Dream

As if to prove the old saying, "Ants and bees build houses to live in; man alone builds a house only to build another," Kirk Kerkorian was not content with the construction of the International Hotel. Even before it was completed he dreamed of building another luxury resort. That facility was the MGM Grand, now known as Bally's.

Kerkorian began construction of the MGM Grand in 1972, with Raquel Welch setting off the first charge of dynamite at the ground-breaking ceremony. Dean Martin provided the entertainment at the grand opening on December 5, 1973.

The MGM Grand was 26 stories high, had 2,100 rooms, and cost $106 million to build, which the sale of assets from Kerkorian's MGM Studios helped fund. The decor was patterned after the MGM film *Grand Hotel*. More than 4,000 employees were required to maintain the hotel and grounds; its seven kitchens served 30,000 meals a day. The hotel's casino, 140 yards in length, took over the title as the largest in the world. It had ten oversized craps tables, seventy blackjack tables, six roulette wheels, sixteen poker tables, and three big wheels.

In keeping with its movie image, the hotel featured many stars, including Bobby Darin, Joan Rivers, Englebert Humperdinck, Barry Manilow, and Burt Bacharach. Donn Arden's spectacular "Jubilee!" opened in the 900-seat Ziegfeld Room in April 1974; in five years it had played to 5 million people.

The MGM Grand turned the intersection at Flamingo and the Strip into the most dynamic corner in Las Vegas. The hotel was for a long time considered the top hotel on the Strip. In the mid-1980s Bally's Corporation purchased the MGM Grand from Kerkorian and changed its name. Kerkorian went on to other ventures.

The MGM Grand, now Bally's, during its opening on December 5, 1973. Las Vegas News Bureau

Aerial view of the Las Vegas Strip, May 1978. Las Vegas News Bureau

Sam Boyd, circa 1970.
Nepwork Photos

Benny Binion, circa 1985.
Nepwork Photos

Local Developers

Not all of Las Vegas's development was done with outside money. When gambling was first legalized in Nevada, numerous small-time operators came to Las Vegas. Some put down roots and went on to construct major gaming properties, becoming much loved in the community in the process. One such individual was Sam Boyd.

Boyd was born in Oklahoma in 1910, and while still a teenager, he was running bingo games on a gambling ship anchored off the coast at Long Beach, California. He operated a bingo parlor in Hawaii from 1934 until 1940 and arrived in Las Vegas in 1941 with $30. He got a job dealing penny roulette and purposefully saved about half of his income.

After military service during World War II, Boyd worked his way up to executive positions at the Sahara and the Mint. Along with Frank Scott he built the Union Plaza at the site of the old Union Railroad Station at the head of Fremont Street in 1971 and formed the Boyd Group, chaired by his son Bill, in 1975. The Boyd Group consisted of hand-picked investors who were Boyd's friends and associates.

In 1975 the Boyd Group constructed the California Hotel and in 1979, Sam's Town. In 1983 the group purchased the Stardust and the Fremont. Boyd died in 1993.

Another individual who came to Las Vegas in the 1940s and rose to heights in the gaming industry was Benny Binion. Binion was born in Texas in 1904 and was a bootlegger and a back-alley gambler before he moved to Las Vegas in 1946. After buying and then selling two downtown casinos, he purchased the old Apache Hotel and the Eldorado Club on Fremont Street and converted them into the Horseshoe Club. In 1988 he acquired the property next door, the Mint Hotel, and combined the two. The expanded Horseshoe was a family-owned hotel and casino, and it encompassed an entire block on Fremont Street.

Binion's eighty-third birthday party was held at the Thomas and Mack Arena, cost a half-million dollars, and was attended by 19,000 people. He died in 1988. Control of the Horseshoe remains in the family.

On the night of October 27, 1993, in perhaps the greatest publicity stunt ever in Las Vegas history, 200,000 people gathered on the Strip near the Flamingo as Steve Wynn threw a switch that set the north tower of the Dunes and its famous sign in flames. Moments later, explosions sent them crashing to the earth in a pile of rubble. Most longtime Las Vegas observers mark the event as the symbolic end of the old Las Vegas and the ushering-in of the new Las Vegas, featuring large family-oriented theme resorts. With the change, Las Vegas emerged as the leading tourist destination in the United States, perhaps even in the world. Jeanne S. Howerton and Mirage Resorts, Inc.

CHAPTER 10

A New Image:
The 1980s and Beyond

In 1980 Las Vegas had about 46,000 hotel and motel rooms and was visited by just under 12 million people. A decade later, in 1990, the city featured nearly 74,000 hotel and motel rooms and welcomed almost 21 million visitors. By mid-1996 the number of hotel and motel rooms in Las Vegas had swelled to over 94,000—more than any other single city in the United States, with visitors pouring into town at the rate of 30 million annually.

And no end to the growth is in sight; an additional 24,000 rooms, at an estimated cost of more than $3.2 billion, are scheduled for completion by the end of 1998, with another 37,000 rooms on the drawing boards. Las Vegas, as a travel industry analyst quoted in the *Wall Street Journal* said, was "redefining what travel is all about" (*Las Vegas Review-Journal* 7/31/94). Las Vegas outdistanced Orlando, Florida, in tourist numbers and New York and Chicago in hosting major conventions. Greater Las Vegas's population hurtled above 1 million in 1995, having grown and succeeded far beyond the greatest hopes of its early promoters.

Such phenomenal growth in Las Vegas is being driven by the construction along the Strip of a score of resort hotels that are among the largest in the world, as well as the expansion of a number of existing properties. Las Vegas now features 12 of the 15 largest hotels in the world and 15 of the largest 20. The city's recent success is reflected in one set of economic figures: in 1986 tourists and conventioneers spent approximately $7.5 billion in the Las Vegas area; the figure had almost tripled to $20.7 million a decade later, in 1995.

Las Vegas's newest resorts have been designed to provide visitors with a fantasy experience. The hotels and their surroundings are constructed around themes that transport visitors to a different realm—for example, a medieval castle, an island in the South Seas, a luxurious hotel in Italy or Monte Carlo, or a pyramid in ancient Egypt.

After a short period in the early 1990s when some Las Vegas resorts tried to provide fun for the entire family, Las Vegas now focuses on what it does best— entertain adults.

Modern History: Excalibur and Luxor

On June 19, 1990, Circus Circus Enterprises, acknowledging the tremendous potential of a resort based on a theme or concept, opened the Excalibur Hotel and Casino. Costing more than $300 million, with construction completed in only nineteen months, Excalibur is a theme resort based on a medieval castle and court. Corporation President William G. Bennett wanted a resort where guests could find pure escapism; he pondered the theme for the Excalibur for seven years before starting the project.

The Excalibur's four 28-story masonry towers contain a total of 4,023 rooms; each room has beds with ornate headboards, wallpaper patterned to resemble castle walls, and window treatments with a royal insignia. Enclosed within the four towers is a casino the size of four football fields, with 2,600 state-of-the-art slot machines and 100 gaming tables. Guests strolling through the 25,000-square-foot shopping and browsing space encounter gypsy wagons, minstrels, and a medieval barge.

Elaborately staged dinner shows in the 900-seat King Arthur's Arena feature fireworks and laser lights in addition to fighting, jousting, and acrobatics by actors in period costumes. A medieval village is re-created on the second level, and the third level houses a wedding chapel; period costumes can be rented for wedding ceremonies.

The Excalibur opened on June 19, 1990, accelerating the city's development of resorts as vacation spots for the entire family. Nearly 11 million people pass through the hotel and casino yearly.
Nepwork Photos

Luxor, Circus Circus Enterprise's $375-million resort designed around an Egyptian theme, opened October 15, 1993. It features 2,526 rooms, and its atrium, the world's largest, could accommodate nine Boeing 747s. Luxor Las Vegas

Excalibur has been extremely successful since its opening, with its occupancy rate usually running at 100 percent. An estimated 30,000 people pass through Excalibur every day—the hotel has nearly 11 million visitors a year.

Circus Circus Enterprises opened its third theme resort in Las Vegas on October 15, 1993. The Luxor, a 30-story, bronze-colored pyramid costing $375 million, is located immediately south of the Excalibur on the west side of the Strip. Designed around an Egyptian theme, the Luxor features 2,526 rooms and the world's largest atrium, consisting of 29 million cubic feet of space, in which nine Boeing 747s could be stacked. The atrium houses 100,000 square feet of casino space with more than 2,500 slot machines and three levels of family-oriented attractions. Visitors enter the hotel through a 30-story sphinx. Inclined elevators called "inclinators" carry patrons up each corner of the pyramid's interior.

Three theme areas are located in the atrium: One takes visitors into the past on an archaeological dig; the second goes to New York's Times Square; the third journeys into the future to the year 2300.

Eleven acres of bronze-colored glass make up the sides of the pyramid. Cleaning the windows for opening day was an immense task requiring 65,000 gallons of solvent and 26 people working eight-hour shifts around the clock for 26 days. A beam of light shines up from the top of the pyramid and, with 40 billions of candle power, it is visible to airlines cruising at altitude 250 miles away. Visitors entering Luxor for the first time are assured a never-before-experienced thrill at the first sight of the enormous volume of space enclosed within the innovative structure.

In the meantime, corporate executives did not neglect Circus Circus. On August 23, 1993, Circus Circus opened Grand Slam Canyon, a 5-acre amusement park enclosed under a 350,000-square-foot glass dome containing 8,615 glass panes. Among the $75 million park's attractions are a double-loop roller coaster, a water flume ride, laser tag, animated dinosaurs, and a 68-foot waterfall.

The Mirage opened November 22, 1989. Tourists gather around the hotel's 54-foot-high model volcano each night to view its scheduled eruptions of fire and smoke. Las Vegas News Bureau

Top left: Steve Wynn (left) chairman of the board of the Mirage Corporation, with star illusionists Siegfried (right) and Roy, and one of their white tigers, in front of the Mirage Hotel, 1990.
Las Vegas News Bureau

Steve Wynn's Theme Resorts:
The Mirage and Treasure Island

Steve Wynn may be the most successful businessman in the world with a bachelor's degree in English literature. The son of a small-time bingo parlor operator, he grew up in the East and graduated from Pennsylvania State University. After college he moved to Las Vegas and was befriended by Las Vegas banker E. Parry Thomas, for years one of the few bankers who would invest in Las Vegas resorts. Wynn began investing in the Golden Nugget in 1971 and with Thomas helping by arranging loans, soon acquired control of the casino. After remodeling the Nugget into a luxurious hotel and casino and adding 600 rooms, Wynn turned his attention to Atlantic City in 1980.

In 1987 Wynn sold his interests in his Atlantic City casino and used the profits toward construction of the Mirage. The Mirage opened November 22, 1989, and cost $610 million.

The hotel boasts 3,049 guest rooms in three 30-story towers and features a South Seas theme. There are deluxe and super-deluxe rooms, king parlors, hospitality suites, and six lanai bungalows with private gardens and pools. The five top floors are used exclusively for tower and penthouse suites, accessible through private elevators. The hotel has two ballrooms: the 40,000-square-foot Grand Ballroom and the 20,000-square-foot Ballroom Mirage.

An outdoor volcano surrounded with waterfalls and lagoons erupts with fire and smoke every fifteen minutes and draws large crowds of spectators. The South Seas theme is further promoted by a lush tropical garden in a 90-foot-high, glass-enclosed atrium and a 20,000-gallon, wall-length aquarium.

Illusionists and master showmen Siegfried and Roy, who for years were a fixture at the Frontier, are featured in a Mirage showroom constructed especially for them by Wynn. Their royal white tigers live in a habitat designed to replicate the animals' natural snow-white environment in their native Himalayas. The hotel also features exhibits, video arcades, costumed characters, and dinner shows created just for young audiences.

Under Wynn, who modestly refers to himself as a "corporate hood ornament," the Mirage has been fabulously successful ("A View from the Top," 1991:8). In the first year of operation, $120 million was taken in from slot machines and $125 million from baccarat. More than $250 million of non-casino revenue was generated; rooms had a 90-percent occupancy rate.

On October 27, 1993, Steve Wynn and associates opened Treasure Island, a 2,900-room resort featuring a Caribbean pirate theme. Located at the corner of Spring Mountain and the Strip adjacent to the Mirage, the facility, with its three 36-story towers, cost $430 million. Designed for middle-income visitors, the interior of the resort, with its approximately 100,000-square-foot gaming area, is designed to replicate a pirate city, with balconies lining the walkways and lanterns illuminating what appear to be shadows of pirates moving through the rooms. Treasure Island is accessed from the Strip by means of a long wooden dock traversing the waters of Buccaneer Bay; an enchanting replica of a pirate village has been constructed on the shore of the bay.

The pirate ship *Hispaniola* and the British frigate H.M.S. *Britannia* battle periodically through the day and night, providing a pyrotechnic show equaling the best of Hollywood special effects. Treasure Island's pirate village and dueling ships raise the Las Vegas tradition of spectacular exteriors to new heights.

Treasure Island, which opened October 27, 1993, is Steve Wynn's second major theme resort to be constructed on the Strip. Located immediately to the north of the Mirage, Treasure Island features a pirate motif, with a battle between the pirate ship Hispaniola *and the British frigate H.M.S.* Britannia *enacted throughout the day and night in the lagoon in front of Treasure Island.*
Mirage Resorts, Inc.

MGM Grand Hotel, Casino, and Theme Park, Kirk Kerkorian's billion-dollar mega resort, which opened December 17, 1993. With entertainment for patrons of all ages, the spectacular resort illustrates Las Vegas's evolution from adults-only entertainment mecca to destination resort for the entire family. MGM Grand, Inc.

Kerkorian Rises Again:
MGM Grand Hotel, Casino, and Theme Park

Late in 1990, Kirk Kerkorian, Las Vegas's quintessential resort builder, a man who carries his own suitcases and is likely to leave the limousines to his associates in preference for a late-model sedan, once described as "without a doubt the nicest, finest, kindest man" (Palermo, 1993) acquired property on the southeast corner of the Strip at Tropicana, including the Tropicana golf course and the Marina Hotel. In 1992 construction began on a resort that was, even by Las Vegas standards, gargantuan. When the MGM Grand Hotel, Casino, and Theme Park opened December 17, 1993, a new era in Las Vegas tourism was fully inaugurated. Costing approximately $1 billion, much of it Kerkorian's own money, the resort features a 5,005-room hotel, the world's second largest; a total gaming area of more than 170,000 square feet, the largest gaming floor in the world; more than a score of restaurants; nearly 160,000 square feet of meeting space; parking for 6,000 cars; and a 33-acre theme park.

On the first day it was open to the public, an estimated 65,000 people visited the resort. The resort's operation requires 7,500 employees, all of whom, in keeping with the MGM's Hollywood theme, are known as "cast members."

More than 3,500 slot machines and 170 tables are found in four separate gaming areas, each with its own theme: the Emerald City Casino, with scenes from the *Wizard of Oz*; the Hollywood Casino, with the ambience of the stars; the Monte Carlo Casino, featuring a marble baccarat pit and tuxedo-clad blackjack dealers along with a touch of the French Riviera; and the Sports Casino. Players, including many Asian high-rollers willing to wager from $150,000 to more than $1 million, make up 20 percent of the resort's gaming business.

Two showrooms, with seating for 1000 and 650, feature the world's top entertainment, and a 15,200-seat special events center is available for boxing and for appearances by the biggest stars. Barbara Streisand, who made her debut in Las Vegas in 1972, opened the special events center with a concert New Year's Eve, December 31, 1993, to a celebrity-filled audience reminiscent of the Academy Awards.

The MGM Grand Adventures theme park, replicating a back-lot movie set, features rides, shows, theme streets, restaurants, shops, and entertainment provided by strolling characters. Theme streets include French Street and Olde England Street; rides include the Grand Canyon Rapids, Deep Earth Exploration, and a Backlot River Tour.

Stratosphere: Bob Stupak's Dream Tower

Standing on three immense 264-foot-tall concrete legs, the 1,149-foot-tall Stratosphere Tower reigns as the dominant feature on Las Vegas's changing skyline. The tower and the hotel and casino complex located at its base are the result of one person's dream, proof positive that even in a city as large and rapidly changing as Las Vegas, one person can make a difference. The huge tower located on the Strip just north of Sahara Avenue is a dream come true for flamboyant Las Vegas businessman Bob Stupak, a high school dropout from Pittsburgh. In 1974 Stupak opened Vegas World at the site now occupied by the Stratosphere. Beginning with 15 slot machines and no hotel rooms, and using modern promotional tactics and a lone-wolf management style, Stupak built Vegas World into a property with 1,350 slot machines and 1,000 hotel rooms, with revenues exceeding $100 million annually.

As is so often the case when a person's dreams change and evolve, Bob Stupak did not initially intend to construct what was to become the tallest freestanding observation tower in the United States, the tallest building west of the Mississippi River. His first idea, the germ from which the tower eventually grew, was to construct a large sign to draw attention to Vegas World, one four times as large as the Stardust's display. The concept of a large sign evolved into what Stupak called a "sign and dine" structure, a restaurant placed atop a large sign. Sign and dine in turn evolved into the notion of a huge tower with a restaurant and other facilities at the top.

Construction of the Stratosphere Tower began November 5, 1991, and it was topped off almost exactly four years later. During construction, the old Vegas World Hotel was closed and gutted, and a 1,500-room hotel and casino were erected in its place.

Fireworks mark the grand opening of the Stratosphere, April 29, 1996. Stratosphere

Construction of the Stratosphere was not without travail. The most serious setback occurred in 1993 when Stupak ran short of cash. Not long after his company had made a public stock offering to complete the tower and resort, in August 1993 the federal government halted stock sales after a fire broke out at the top of the unfinished tower. Stupak realized he would need a partner to complete the project and selected Lyle Berman, a poker friend and founder of Grand Casinos, Inc., of Minneapolis. Grand Casinos, a large gaming company formed in 1991 with interests in Mississippi, Minnesota, and Louisiana, had a strong desire to participate in the boom on the Las Vegas Strip and saw a partnership with Stupak as an opportunity to become part owner of a major Strip property for a relatively small amount of money—about $65 million. Since Grand Casinos became involved, Stupak has gradually reduced his investments and role in management of the Stratosphere. Perhaps more important for the future of Las Vegas and its spot on the world's maps, another major setback for Stupak occurred when he proposed the tower's height be substantially increased, making it the tallest structure in the world. In a decision that he says brought him heartache, he was prevented from doing so by officials' concerns for aviation safety, which Stupak maintains were overblown.

The grand opening of the Stratosphere was held April 30, 1996. In addition to the tower, the complex includes a 100,000-square-foot casino and a 160,000-square-foot entertainment and retail space.

A 12-story structure called the "pod" sits at the top of the tower. Four high-speed double-deck elevators move visitors from ground level to observation decks located in the pod in just 30 seconds. Three wedding chapels with appropriately themed decor are located at the top of the tower. The chapels are named Heavenly Garden, Renaissance Court, and Cupid's Terrace. The tower's top also features a 360-seat restaurant that makes a complete revolution every 20 minutes, as well as a 220-seat cocktail lounge. Both offer stunning panoramic views of the city and desert below.

Sitting at the top pod, 900 feet above the street, are two amusement thrill rides—the Let It Ride High Roller and the Big Shot. The High Roller is a roller-coaster that winds around on tracks on the top of the pod. The Big Shot thrusts passengers 160 feet into the air along the mast that extends, needle-like, into the air from the pod's top. One of only three such rides in existence, passengers experience up to four Gs going up, and free-fall back to the launching pad.

View of the Las Vegas Strip looking south from the 1,149-foot-tall Stratosphere Tower, 1996.
Stratosphere

Admirers of the Stratosphere Tower note that all great civilizations build structures and monuments that define them, that proclaim their society's presence to all. Egypt has the pyramids; Athens the Parthenon; Rome the Coliseum; Paris the Eiffel Tower; New York City the Empire State Building; and Chicago the Sears Tower. Many believe the Stratosphere will come to symbolize Las Vegas, defining the city's image as it dominates the skyline.

Monte Carlo: Popular Elegance

When Mirage Resorts, Inc., chairman Steve Wynn toured the $344 million Monte Carlo Resort and Casino just prior to its grand opening on June 21, 1996, he proclaimed, "This is popular elegance" (Palermo, 1996). The resort and casino are modeled after the famous Palais du Casino at Monte Carlo, the largest of five areas in the tiny principality of Monaco (0.75 square miles in size). Monaco, situated on the coast of the Mediterranean Sea, is a few miles east of Nice, France, near the Italian border. *Monte* means "hill" in Italian, and *Carlo* is Italian for "Charles." The famous casino is named after Prince Charles III, who gave Monaco its independence in 1861. With its arches, chandeliers, gas-lighted promenades, statues of cherubs, stained glass skylights, and marble-floored bathrooms complete with brass fixtures, Las Vegas's Monte Carlo is an effort to provide visitors with some of the ambience and style of its renowned namesake.

The Monte Carlo, 32 stories tall and holding 3,014 rooms, is the seventh-largest hotel in the world, outdistancing substantially the total of 2,500 hotel rooms found in all of Monaco. The huge hotel is the result of a joint venture between Mirage Resorts, Inc., and Gold Strike Resorts, which operated casinos in Jean and Henderson, Nevada. Before the Monte Carlo was completed, Gold Strike Resorts merged with Circus Circus. Mirage Resorts put up 44 acres of land that had originally been part of the site of the old Dunes and $20 million in cash, and Circus Circus anted up $67 million. An additional $210 million was obtained by the two companies to complete the project.

The resort was built, under budget, in a mere 14 months; this speed was possible because Circus Circus's internal construction company, Circus Circus Development, served as the general contractor. Circus Circus will manage the property, and the two partners will split the net revenues 50-50. Revenues are predicted to range between $32 and $80 million annually.

The Monte Carlo's 90,000-square-foot casino is equipped with 2,200 slot machines, 95 table games, a race and sports book, a poker room, a keno lounge, and a 550-seat bingo room. The resort features 5 restaurants, a 210-seat food court, a beer hall, and a microbrewery designed to produce 10,000 barrels of 6 different beers per year. Magician Lance Burton has been signed to a 13-year contract, and a 1,200-seat, $27 million Victorian-style theater, inspired by venues in London's West End (and including a $1.5 million sound system), has been constructed for his show. A nearly 1/2-acre pool area, with more than 11,000 square feet of water surface, cost $2.5 million and is a favorite feature at the resort. The area includes a 4,800-square-foot wave pool with gently sloping shallows to simulate a beach and 5 different types of waves that change every 15 minutes.

Because of the expense involved in creation of new hotel-casinos, many analysts see a trend toward more joint ventures on the Strip in the future.

Grand opening of the Monte Carlo Resort and Casino, June 21, 1996. Monte Carlo Resort and Casino

New York–New York: The Big Apple in Las Vegas

New York–New York Hotel and Casino sits on 18 acres of highly prized real estate located on the northwest corner of the intersection at Tropicana Avenue and the Strip. Its opening in January 3, 1997 completed the metamorphosis of a corner that only a few years earlier had been somewhat isolated at the far south end of the Strip. Now the intersection is the city's entertainment center of gravity. All that was required for the transformation was inspiration, willingness to take a chance, and the investment of a couple of billion dollars.

New York–New York is, as the name implies, an effort to re-create the best of the Big Apple's images and ambience in a Las Vegas–style resort. In the early 1990s financier Kirk Kerkorian, who has, along with Steve Wynn of Mirage Resorts, Inc., and Bill Bennett at Circus Circus, Inc., reigned for years as one of Las Vegas's quintessential resort creators, optioned the 18 acres of vacant land that New York–New York now occupies. At the time Steve Wynn, who had recently obtained the old Dunes Hotel and golf course, also tried to obtain the property, but failed.

Later, Kerkorian entered into a joint venture with Gary E. Primm and his Primadonna Resorts, Inc., which owns and operates three highly successful casino and hotel resorts on the Nevada-California border on Interstate 15 some 40 miles south of Las Vegas. Kerkorian put up his 18 acres, and Primadonna, Inc., put up $42 million in cash, with the balance needed to construct the $460 million facility obtained as a commercial bank loan.

Architecturally, New York–New York is probably the most unique and interesting building to be erected in Las Vegas, rivaled only by the pyramid-shaped Luxor. The exterior consists of 12 adjoining skyscraper towers with distinct facades that replicate famous New York City buildings, including the Chrysler

New York–New York just prior to its opening, January 3, 1997. Jeanne S. Howerton

Building, the Century Building, the Lever House Soap Company Building, and the CBS Building. The structure is topped off by the 510 feet (47 stories) of the Empire State Building replica, making it the tallest building in Las Vegas. Guests occupying the hotel's 2,035 rooms and suites get to their quarters through four main elevator banks located in each of the four highest towers. In keeping with the spirit of New York City, a 50-foot-high, 150-foot replica of the Statue of Liberty stands in front of the hotel, along with a 300-foot-long replica of the Brooklyn Bridge, which serves as the walkway entrance. Evoking memories of Coney Island at the turn of the century is the Manhattan Express, the world's first roller-coaster to feature a "heartline" twist-and-dive maneuver, producing a sensation like that felt by a pilot doing a barrel roll in an airplane (the center of rotation becomes the same as the passenger's center of gravity). Passengers will board the thrill ride inside the casino—a 144-foot drop at 67 miles per hour plummets passengers to within a few feet of the hotel's valet entrance.

The resort's interior further accentuates the New York City theme. The 84,000-square-foot casino is broken into theme areas. It features 75 gaming tables and more than 2,400 slot machines. The Financial District is the casino cashier's cage. The sports book resembles a historic race track. Central Park includes the central casino gaming area, and Park Avenue is lined with retail shops inside elegant facades. Penn Station and Grand Central Station overlook the casino play area. The registration area greets guests with a large diorama of Manhattan's nighttime skyline. A variety of foods is available at themed restaurants, including Italian, Chinese, and Continental, and there is a food court along with several nightclubs and pubs. Guest rooms feature 63 different decor themes. Carpet pathways in the casino carry the design of an authentic New York street, complete with curbs and crosswalks, to guide visitors.

Fremont Street Experience: Help for Downtown

Fremont Street in downtown Las Vegas has recently undergone a massive transformation. Automobile access along 5 blocks of Glitter Gulch has been permanently eliminated. A 90-foot-high space frame has been constructed above the street to serve as a platform for a light and sound show featuring 2.1 million lights and a 540,000-watt sound system. The $70 million project, known as the Fremont Street Experience, opened in December 1995. It is an unprecedented public-private partnership between the city of Las Vegas and the Fremont Street Experience Company, a group of 11 downtown hotels—Binion's Horseshoe, California, El Cortez, Fitzgerald's, Four Queens, Fremont, Golden Gate, Golden Nugget, Jackie Gaughan's Plaza, Las Vegas Club, and Main Street Station. Funding for development was provided by hotel members and hotel room taxes, city redevelopment funds, the Las Vegas Convention Visitors Authority, and gasoline and transportation taxes. Operating expenses are provided by member hotels. The project was intended to help revitalize the flagging fortunes of downtown Las Vegas, which has not kept pace with growth on the Strip in recent years. Early returns suggest an increase in visitor numbers to what some old-timers call the Street of Dreams.

The Fremont Street Experience, 1996, showing the conversion of Fremont Street in downtown Las Vegas into a pedestrian mall featuring an extravagant light and sound show. Fremont Street Experience

Artist's representation of Mirage Resorts, Inc.'s Bellagio, a $1.25 billion resort hotel under construction at the site of the Dunes Hotel at the intersection of the Strip and Flamingo Road. Scheduled to open in spring 1998, Mirage Resorts chairman Steve Wynn promises the Bellagio will be "the most beautiful hotel in the world." Mirage Resorts, Inc.

Bellagio: Steve Wynn Does It Again

Rising like a phoenix on the site of the old Dunes Hotel on the southwest corner of the Strip and Flamingo Road is Bellagio, the newest creation of Steve Wynn's Mirage Resorts, Inc. The $1.25 billion resort hotel, the most expensive ever in Las Vegas, promises to do for Las Vegas in the late 1990s what Wynn's Mirage did for the town in the late 1980s—set a new standard for quality and excellence.

Construction of Bellagio began in late 1995 and is scheduled to open in spring 1998. Wynn promises the resort will be the "single most captivating hotel on earth" (Green, 1996). The 35-story, 3,000-room hotel was inspired by the idyllic village of Bellagio, overlooking northern Italy's beautiful Lake Como. The hotel will be set back 450 feet from the Strip alongside an 11-acre version of Lake Como. A $30 million choreographed water ballet will shoot streams of water 160 feet into the air and will be Bellagio's signature, just as the Mirage's volcano and Treasure Island's pirate battle are signatures for those hotels.

Ambience will be relaxed but sophisticated, with extensive use of picture windows throughout to allow guests to enjoy romantic vistas of lushly landscaped grounds. Rooms will be decorated with European antiques and artwork and will feature separate showers and bathtubs with extensive use of imported marble. Food served by internationally acclaimed restaurateurs, upscale boutiques, and a $70 million production created by the Cirque du Soleil will add to the Bellagio experience. A monorail will connect Bellagio with the Monte Carlo.

Bellagio's setting of a new standard for elegance, luxury, and creativity will likely ratchet up the competition level for other resort operators and, as with the Mirage, further redefine the city's image as a place to visit and have fun.

The Boom Continues

The frantic pace of construction of new resorts—and the expansion of existing ones—aimed at Las Vegas visitors continues. Soon it will be a short walk from New York to Paris. The owners of Bally's Las Vegas, which is located at the intersection of Flamingo Road and the Strip, plan to construct a $500 million hotel casino on 25 acres adjoining Bally's on the south. Named Paris Casino-Resort, it is slated to have 3,000 rooms, an 85,000-square-foot casino, and a 1,500-seat showroom. Among its attractions will be a 50-story replica of the Eiffel Tower and likenesses of the Arc de Triomphe, the Champs Elysées, the Paris Opéra, the River Seine, and a French-themed shopping complex resembling a Paris street.

Circus-Circus Enterprises, Inc., owners of megaresorts Circus Circus, Excalibur, and Luxor in Las Vegas, own a contiguous mile on the west side of the Strip between Tropicana and Russell Road. The Excalibur, the Luxor, and the Hacienda are located on that property. The company's Masterplan Mile calls for further ambitious development of the site. The company expects eventually to own or control as many as 20,000 hotel rooms on the Masterplan Mile. The Hacienda Hotel and Casino was demolished on New Year's Eve, 1996, and a 4,000-room resort costing $800 million will be constructed at the site. It is scheduled to open in late 1998. Connected to—but separate from—the megasized hotel and casino will be a stand-alone 400-room luxury Four Seasons Hotel, the first five-star facility in Las Vegas. Four Seasons Resort Hotels and Resorts is the world's largest operator of luxury hotels.

Luxor Las Vegas, the Strip's distinctive pyramid-shaped resort, has undergone a $240 million expansion. Two 22-story stepped towers forming a pyramid have added 1,940 rooms to the existing 2,526 total, making it (for a time, at least) the third largest hotel in the world. North of Masterplan Mile on the Strip, Circus Circus has been expanded with construction of a 35-story tower costing $60 million, adding 1,000 rooms to that property. It is now the fifth largest hotel in the world.

The Sands Hotel Casino closed permanently on June 30, 1996. Plans call for two 3,000-unit all-suite hotels, with 100,000-square-foot casinos and a 500,000-square-foot upscale shopping mall to be built in its place. The project will feature a Venetian theme, with extensive waterways, canals,

Artist's representation of Paris Casino-Resort set for construction by the Bally Entertainment Corporation on 25 acres located on the Strip between Bally's Las Vegas and the Aladdin Hotel and Casino. Bally Entertainment Corporation

Artist's representation of the resort to be built at the site of the Sands at an estimated cost of $1.5 billion. The first phase of construction is scheduled for completion in late 1998. Sands Hotel/Casino and Convention Center

Master-plan model of the $900 million expansion program at Caesars Palace. ITT Corporation

and elegant finishes. The estimated cost of the project is $1.5 billion, and the first phase is scheduled for completion in late 1998.

Down the street, the Desert Inn, once the tallest building on the Strip, is slated for a $160 million facelift and conversion to a five-star resort hotel, casino, and golf course. On 34 acres adjacent to the Desert Inn, ITT Sheraton, owner of both the Desert Inn and Caesars Palace, plans to spend $850 million on a 3,200-room resort named Planet Hollywood.

Caesars Palace is undergoing a $900 million expansion that will include a major facelift and the eventual construction of 2,100 additional upscale rooms and suites. A tower containing 1,100 rooms comparable in luxury to those in Bellagio is scheduled to be completed in late 1997. The Forum Shops at Caesars, the most successful retail center in the nation in terms of annual sales per square foot (the industry average is about $300 per square foot, with between $400 and $700 considered extremely successful; the Forum Shops average $1,200) will more than double its size.

Down the street, the Aladdin, which in recent years has benefited enormously from the construction of new resorts at the south end of the Strip, has been given the go-ahead by county commissioners for a $600 million expansion and renovation that will more than double the number of rooms to a total of 2,600 and will create a 500,000-square-foot shopping mall while preserving the futuristic Arabian theme.

In late 1995 William G. Bennett, former head of Circus Circus Enterprises, purchased both the Sahara Hotel and the site, now vacant, of the old El Rancho Vegas. Bennett, whose credits include the Excalibur and the Luxor, will perform a facelift, add a 1,300-room tower, and double the casino size.

Harrah's is spending $150 million to add 694 rooms and 22,000 feet to its casino. The facade will be changed from a riverboat theme to one based on Mardi Gras and Carnival. These improvements are scheduled to be completed in spring 1997.

An operator of two New Jersey racetracks has announced that the shuttered El Rancho, formerly the Thunderbird, will be transformed at a cost of $1 billion into the Star Ship Orion, designed to resemble a spaceship. Plans call for 2,400 rooms, including a 65-story, 1,400-room luxury hotel.

These announced projects are only highlights of the construction planned in Las Vegas. Scores of other projects on the drawing boards or underway in the valley would draw considerable attention in most communities not undergoing such rapid transformation.

Move Over, Broadway

The El Rancho Vegas, which opened April 3, 1941, was the first Las Vegas hotel to use big-name entertainers to attract crowds and high-rollers. From this modest beginning, Las Vegas's much-deserved reputation as an entertainment mecca has grown. The names of the biggest stars have lit up the Strip's marquees—the pizazz of Broadway has melded with Hollywood's glamour on the desert in southern Nevada.

Never resting on its laurels, the entertainment promised Las Vegas visitors has continued its spectacular evolution. As Hollywood film producers turned increasingly to special effects to tell their stories, notably in such popular films as *Star Wars* (1977), *Raiders of the Lost Ark* (1981), and *Jurassic Park* (1993), the producers of Las Vegas's big shows were impressed by the power of special effects on audiences. Increasingly, special effects have been incorporated into huge new productions, with each new show being more spectacular than the last—and more expensive. In 1990, Siegfried and Roy upped the ante at the Mirage with their $28 million, as *Time* magazine put it, "farrago of illusion and sorcery" (April 24, 1995). That was followed at Treasure Island by Cirque du Soleil's $33 million Mystère. In 1995, the MGM Grand Hotel raised the stakes to astonishing levels with its $68 million production of *EFX,* including $27 million to equip its Grand Theater with 3-D movie projection, hot-wired rumble seats, and a "fog wall" of steam and liquid nitrogen. Given the huge sums involved in producing such spectaculars, most industry observers believe it unlikely that Broadway will be able to compete in the future with Las Vegas in both quantity and quality of big shows. Move over, New York, Las Vegas is the new show capital of the world!

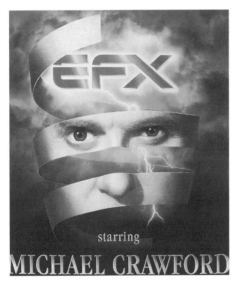

Michael Crawford, who starred in the MGM Grand Hotel's spectacular EFX, from its opening in March, 1995, until he left the show in August, 1996. At a cost of $68 million, EFX exemplifies how Las Vegas shows have become increasingly more spectacular, showcasing the biggest names in show business and utilizing the very latest in computer and special-effects technology. David Cassidy replaced Michael Crawford. MGM Grand, Inc.

Cast of Andrew Lloyd Webber's Starlight Express, *featured at the Las Vegas Hilton, 1995. The Hilton showroom, originally built with Elvis Presley in mind, was reconstructed in 1993 to accommodate the* Starlight Express. *Costumes weigh up to 45 pounds and cost between $10,000 and $20,000 each. Such shows enable Las Vegas to maintain its grip on the title "Entertainment Capital of the World."* Las Vegas Hilton

LAS VEGAS

Neighborhood Casinos

As Las Vegas has grown, so have the opportunities for smaller resorts, located away from both the Strip and downtown; these operations cater to local gamers as well as out-of-town visitors. Beginning in 1954, the Showboat was the first to demonstrate that a large resort could be profitable although not located either downtown or on the Strip. Sam's Town opened in 1979 about four miles south of the Showboat on the Boulder Highway, further proving that an outlying resort could be successful. The Bingo Palace (renamed the Palace Station in 1984) was constructed about a mile west of the Strip on Sahara by Frank Fertitta, Jr., in 1976. It was the first important casino to cater almost exclusively to the local market. In 1986, Michael Gaughan, son of Jackie Gaughan, (who began a long career of casino operation and ownership when he came to Las Vegas in 1943 and at one time or another held an interest in such places as the Flamingo, El Cortez, and Union Plaza), built the Gold Coast about 1 mile west of the Strip on Flamingo. In 1990, the Rio opened across the street from the Gold Coast, and in 1991 the Santa Fe, featuring an ice-skating rink, opened at the north end of the Las Vegas Valley on Rancho Drive. The Boulder Station, located on the Boulder Highway, and Boomtown Hotel-Casino, & RV Resort situated at I-15 and Blue Diamond, opened in 1994. About one-half mile east of the Strip on Harmon, the $88 million Hard Rock Hotel opened in 1995; though located off-Strip, it caters primarily to visitors. All of these establishments have been immensely successful. Additionally, more than a dozen neighborhood resorts are either planned or under construction.

The Bingo Palace, circa 1980, and signs from several Las Vegas neighborhood casinos, 1995.
Las Vegas News Bureau and R. McCracken

Hollywood filmmakers recognized very early that Las Vegas, with its unique lifestyle, architecture, and surrounding desert, made a fine location for shooting films. Here, One Million B.C. *is being filmed in the Valley of Fire by Hal Roach Studios in 1940.* University of Nevada, LasVegas–Dickinson Library Special Collections

Roll 'Em: On Location in Las Vegas

With its desert and mountain vistas, abundant sunshine, ample lodging facilities, and unique architecture and lifestyle, Las Vegas has long been a favorite location for filmmakers. A motion picture titled *Hazards of Helen* was shot in Las Vegas in 1915, and Hal Roach made at least two films there in the 1920s, one called *Rex, King of the Wild Horses. One Million B.C.*, starring Victor Mature and Lon Chaney, was filmed near Las Vegas in 1940, and Roy Rogers and Dale Evans filmed *Helldorado* in town in 1946. In 1952 Victor Mature was back in Las Vegas with co-star Jane Russell for the film noir classic, *The Las Vegas Story*.

With all the money floating around Las Vegas it was only natural that films about stealing it would be made, including *They Came to Rob Las Vegas* (1959), starring Jack Palance and Lee J. Cobb, and *Ocean's 11* (1960), starring Frank Sinatra and the "Rat Pack." Elvis Presley's *Viva Las Vegas* (1964) and Robert Redford's *The Electric Horseman* (1979) were also set in Las Vegas. Francis Ford Coppola's *One From the Heart* (1987), which was set in Las Vegas, was filmed on a Hollywood sound stage, but it looked more like Las Vegas than the real thing.

Beginning in the 1980s the state of Nevada began to actively promote the state as a site for the filming of movies. These efforts led to increasing use of Las Vegas as a filmmaking location. Businesses in Las Vegas and southern Nevada that supply and provide services to filmmakers grew as a result; these businesses include caterers, crane operators, gaming consultants, and those providing airline charters, mobile phones, lighting equipment, and tents. The management of the Las Vegas Hilton actively recruited movie and production companies.

Twenty-nine national commercials were shot in the Las Vegas area in 1990. In recent years such movies as *Cherry 2000*, *Lost in America*, *Rainman*, *Honeymoon in Las Vegas*, *Leaving Las Vegas*, Martin Scorsese's *Casino*, and *Vegas Vacation* have been filmed in the city. In addition to adding to southern Nevada's economy, film and television exposure is worth millions of dollars in promotion for Las Vegas and its glamorous lifestyle.

The Las Vegas Story, *produced by Howard Hughes and starring Victor Mature and Jane Russell, was filmed in Las Vegas. The world premiere was held at El Portal Theater on Fremont Street in 1952.* Las Vegas News Bureau

Elvis Presley and bride Priscilla Beaulieu cutting their wedding cake, May 1, 1967, at the Aladdin Hotel in Las Vegas. Though he had performed in Las Vegas in 1956 and starred in the movie Viva Las Vegas *in 1964, Elvis was not closely identified with Las Vegas until the 1970s.* Nepwork Photos

The futuristic movie Cherry 2000 *was shot in and around Las Vegas in 1985. In the film, the casinos on the Las Vegas Strip had been abandoned and buried in sand dunes. Here Bambi McCracken, who appeared in the film, stands in front of a casino sign sticking out of the sand.* Author's photo collection

Exterior of the Dunes Hotel, looking toward the west, circa 1980. Las Vegas News Bureau

11

In Remembrance

Through the years many hotels and casinos have opened in Las Vegas. With proper management a large percentage have thrived, changing and growing with the times. Yet Las Vegas also has had its hotel and casino casualties—properties, at times among the once most glamorous in town, that for one reason or another failed to remain open. Sometimes they closed and were torn down because a builder had other plans for the site, as with the Pair-O-Dice, where the Last Frontier was constructed, or the Castaways, where the Mirage was built. The old El Rancho Vegas, the first resort constructed on what eventually became the Strip, burned down in 1960 and was never rebuilt.

Poor management and resulting lack of profitability led to the closure of two of Las Vegas's biggest casualties: the Dunes and the Landmark.

The Dunes

The most spectacular resort failure in Las Vegas's history was the Dunes. For nearly thirty years the Dunes was one of the most important and prestigious resorts on the Strip. When it opened on May 23, 1955, on the southwest corner of Flamingo and Las Vegas Boulevard, it was the southernmost hotel on the Strip.

The Dunes featured an Arabian Nights motif and was known for its fiber-glass statue of a thirty-foot sultan standing with his arms akimbo at the entrance to the casino. The sultan later was moved to the Dunes golf course adjoining Interstate 15, where for many years he welcomed travelers to Las Vegas.

The Dunes, Riviera, and Royal Nevada (a small hotel located on a side street off the Strip) all opened within a few months of one another; at that time there

The Dunes Hotel, complete with its famous statue of an Arabian sultan, circa 1955. Nepwork Photos

was not enough business to support three new establishments. The competition was especially bad for the owners of the Dunes, who were East- and West-Coast businessmen with no gaming experience. The resort ran into financial trouble, and for a time the casino was closed and the Dunes operated solely as a hotel.

Shortly after, the property was bought by Jake Gottlieb, owner of a Chicago shipping company, who was rumored to have mob associations. He hired Major Arteburn Riddle to turn the Dunes around. Riddle was something of a marketing genius and is said to have made several key innovations that made the hotel profitable.

Riddle first decided to book Minsky's Follies, starring Lou Costello, for a six-week run. The review, which featured bare-breasted showgirls and created controversy, was an immediate success. Minsky's stayed at the Dunes for four and a half years. The successor to Minsky's was Casino de Paris, which played for over twenty years.

Riddle's second innovation was to open the Sultan's Table, the first genuine gourmet restaurant in Las Vegas and the only restaurant in the history of the Diner's Club to have the distinction of being named "America's finest and most beautiful new restaurant" (Stamos, 1979d:8).

Next Riddle initiated construction of an 18-hole, 72-par golf course on property immediately south of the Dunes. He also increased lodging capacity, raising the hotel's room total from 194 to 450. By this time Riddle had purchased the hotel from Gottlieb.

LAS VEGAS

Floyd Patterson, pictured with writer Norman Mailer and performer Judy Garland, July 17, 1963, five days before his title fight with Sonny Liston. Patterson's training camp was located in the Dunes Hotel. Las Vegas News Bureau

In 1965 a 24-story high-rise was completed. This addition pushed the Dunes's room total to over 1,000. The hotel's familiar sign, "Diamond of the Dunes," was erected to mark the occasion, at a cost of $318,000. It was then the largest free-standing sign in the world.

The Dunes prospered through the 1970s, but in the 1980s it changed hands several times and suffered from mismanagement and debt. It was purchased by a Japanese millionaire in 1988 and sold to Steve Wynn and the Mirage Corporation in 1992. It was permanently closed in 1993, the first truly big hotel in the heart of the Strip to fold.

On October 27, 1993, 200,000 people gathered on the Strip to say goodbye to the Dunes. At precisely 10:10 P.M., in what was Las Vegas's most spectacular show, the 28-year-old, 18-story diamond sign and nearby hotel tower were dynamited and, in the blink of an eye, both collapsed in a heap of rubble. The Dunes's explosion was choreographed, beginning with $1 million worth of fireworks set off over a period of six minutes, followed by an imaginary volley from the pirate ship anchored at Treasure Island, at which time the front of the tower and all 24 floors of the old structure were engulfed in flames. Then came the low rumble of dynamite exploding, and the Dunes was destroyed. A new era in Las Vegas history had begun.

The Sands

The closing of the Sands Hotel Casino on June 30, 1996, left an empty feeling in the many people who knew and loved Las Vegas in decades past. Comedian Bob Newhart played the Sands's fabulous Copa Room and credits an engagement there as the time "when I became a stand-up comic for real" (Green, 1996). Upon hearing the news that the Sands was closing, he said, "A piece of me died."

For decades the Sands was known for an atmosphere highly conducive to relaxation and having fun. Architects say that part of the secret was its architecture, and credit its original architect, Wayne McAllister, who invented the idea of a luxury Strip hotel when he designed the El Rancho Vegas in 1941. The Sands Tower, designed in 1965 by Martin Stern, Jr., preserved the relaxed tradition and was, it is said, "a rebuke of the boxy towers of today…a magnificent piece of suburban architecture" (Hess, 1996). In the Sands, architect-critic Alan Hess contends, the suburban architectural form, with its low rambling buildings, cool green lawns, ever-present pool, and easy acceptance of the automobile, reached its full potential as a place to relax and mingle, to see and be seen—as its marquee once proclaimed, "A Place In The Sun." As the Sands fades into history, Hess fears Las Vegas is on the verge of being "Manhattanized."

The Sands Hotel circa 1968. With entertainers such as Frank Sinatra (described as the "Lord and Master of Show Business, Las Vegas–Style") and Count Basie in the Copa Room, the Sands, the seventh resort constructed on the Strip, was in its glory as the "in" place in Las Vegas. Las Vegas News Bureau.

During the 1950s and 1960s the Sands reigned as the "in" place in Las Vegas. It was packed with fun-seekers from all walks of life who rubbed elbows with celebrities. Frank Sinatra and the Rat Pack could be found holding court at the Sands. The audiences in the showrooms and lounge were hip. "They dug everything we did," Joey Bishop recalled. "I don't ever remember, in my life, performers so anxious to go to work. We couldn't wait to go to work," he remarked when interviewed at the time of the Sands's closing.

Although the sense of glamour and excitement at the Sands diminished somewhat during the 1970s and 1980s, the resort continued until the early 1990s to be one of the jewels on the Strip—still bright, still providing a little thrill when a visitor walked through the front door. But when the Mirage opened across the Strip in late 1989 and the era of the megaresort began, the venerable establishment became increasingly less able to compete for visitors who had never known—or had forgotten—what it had been. Its fate was sealed; the Sands was shut down to make room for another megaresort.

The Last Roll of the Dice

The Sands closed its doors to the public forever at 6:00 P.M. on June 30, 1996. At 5:00 P.M. casino officials began cordoning off banks of slot machines and closing the gaming tables where two generations of celebrities and common folk alike had tried their luck. By 5:50 P.M. most of the slots were sealed off; five minutes later they were all down. At 3 minutes to 6:00 one roulette wheel and one craps table were still operating. With a short minute to go they closed the roulette table. A small crowd remained on the casino floor, milling about, ill at ease, most staying near the craps table, perhaps trying to fix in memory what they were experiencing—the lights, the sounds, even the smells—one more moment of excitement with an old friend. CNN and other news outfits were there with their $40,000 Sony television cameras, shooting footage for the obituary.

The Sands marquee the night it closed, June 30, 1996. Jeanne S. Howerton.

Suddenly a buzz went through the crowd. A man who appeared to be about 50 years old was working his way through the crowd toward the craps table. Flanked by two bodyguards walking slightly behind him, he was shorter than average, dressed in dark slacks and an expensive silk shirt with a black and white floral design, worn open at the collar. People turned and watched as the man walked past them. As he approached the craps table, the dealers recognized him, and they spoke, nodding and smiling politely. It was Bob Stupak, the Stratosphere's owner and a legendary gambler, a man who once bet $1 million on the Superbowl.

As they talked, Stupak reached into his pocket and pulled out an enormous stack of $100 bills at least an inch and a half thick. He peeled five bills off the top and dropped them on the "don't pass" line on the craps table. The shooter at the other end of the table made his point. Stupak lost and the dealer picked up the bills. Stupak then methodically peeled off 15 more $100 bills and placed them on the "don't pass" line. The shooter rolled the dice—snake eyes; he had crapped out. Fifteen hundred dollars richer, Stupak picked up his bet and his winnings.

Then, without saying a word, one of the dealers reached under the craps table and pulled out the plastic-and-wooden lid used to cover a craps table's chips when the table is not in use. Carefully he and another dealer set the lid in place. The last gaming table at the Sands was now apparently closed. The crowd began to stir, most wondering what they should do now. Was it over? Some began milling around again. Stupak remained at the craps table talking to the people in the pit.

It was now two or three minutes past 6:00 P.M. Unexpectedly, one of the dealers began removing the lid that had only moments before been placed on the craps table. Stupak, who had been standing in the pit, moved to the end of the table and reached into his pocket for his wad, pulled it out, peeled off 10 "Bens," as the hookers call them (for Benjamin Franklin), and, with a snappy motion of his wrist, tossed them down onto number 4. The dealer quickly removed the bills from the table and replaced them with two $500 chips.

Stupak, holding a cigarette in one hand, took the dice in the other and began shaking them, pausing several times to blow on them. After shaking the dice for the longest time, he let them fly. For a moment the dice seemed to hold, frozen in the air, then fell onto the green felt. Stupak had missed his point. The dealer picked up the two $500 chips and placed them on the $500-chip stack. He reached under the table for the lid and began setting it in place. That was the last roll of dice at the Sands. The casino was closed. The old Las Vegas was gone.

Top. At 2 A.M., November 26, 1996, detonation of explosives placed at strategic locations in the famous tower of the Sands Hotel on the Las Vegas Strip sent it crashing to the ground. This sequence of photos taken from across the street shows the tower as smoke from the blasts first appears; the venerable symbol of Las Vegas celebrity then crumples into a pile of dust and rubble. Lou Fox

Bottom. Two weeks after the detonation of the Sands tower, the rubble has been cleared. Looking toward the northwest, the wreckage of the crashed C-123 cargo plane used in filming the movie Con Air *is visible in the foreground. Heavy equipment can be seen removing the foundation which once supported the seventeen-story tower.* Jeanne S. Howerton

The Landmark

The Landmark was started by Frank Caroll, a Kansas City builder, in 1961. Designed as a tower with a dome at the top, the hotel was initially intended to have 14 stories. As a result of a contest with the Mint Hotel downtown for the status of Nevada's tallest building, the Landmark was eventually pushed to 31 stories.

Caroll encountered financial difficulties and was not able to finish construction of the hotel. Howard Hughes purchased the property in 1968 for $17 million, completed the hotel, and opened it on July 2, 1969.

Several years later, Hughes conveyed the property to actress Jean Peters as part of their divorce settlement. It subsequently changed hands several times and was permanently closed in 1991. It was imploded December 7, 1995. No new structure has been erected at the site.

The Landmark, pictured shortly after its opening July 2, 1969, was completed by Howard Hughes and closed permanently in 1991. It now stands empty and is scheduled for demolition. Las Vegas News Bureau

LAS VEGAS

The Moulin Rouge opened in May 1955 and closed six months later due to insufficient capital. Located on Las Vegas's west side, it is best remembered for offering gambling opportunities to all races, since no other Las Vegas casino-hotel was then open on a regular basis to black patrons.
Las Vegas News Bureau

The Silver Slipper, seen here in 1975, was built in 1942 as part of the Last Frontier's Western Village; it was turned into the Silver Slipper in 1950. The casino closed November 28, 1988, and was torn down by the present owners of the Frontier. The site has been converted into a parking lot.
Las Vegas News Bureau

The Sans Souci opened October 23, 1957, changed its name to the Castaways in 1964, and closed in July 1987 to make room for construction of the Mirage. Pictured here in 1970, the Castaways was located across the Strip from the Sands and sat approximately where the Mirage's volcano now stands. At one time Howard Hughes owned both the Castaways and the Silver Slipper.
Las Vegas News Bureau

The Hacienda

The Hacienda opened at the far south end of the Strip in June 1956. Built by Warren "Doc" Bayley and his wife, Judy, who owned a chain of motels in California by the same name, the Hacienda was initially denied a gaming license by state officials who used the excuse that the new casino would not be missed because the Strip was already overbuilt. Because of its isolated location, the Hacienda survived on promotions. During the 1960s it operated a fleet of 30 airplanes to bring in customers. Consistently profitable through the years, the Hacienda was imploded on New Year's Eve, 1996, and a 4,000-room, $800 million megaresort will be constructed in its place by Circus Circus Enterprises, Inc. The new resort is scheduled to open in late 1998.

The Hacienda Hotel and Casino, 1996.
Circus Circus Enterprises.

The Hacienda Hotel when it opened in June 1956.
Nepwork Photo.

Epilogue

With the opening of half a dozen of the world's largest resort hotels in the 1990s, Las Vegas's metamorphosis from a town with a somewhat naughty image catering to adults to a blue-ribbon vacation destination providing elaborate fantasy-oriented attractions was complete. Although gaming is still a key to resort operations, it is packaged as part of an unmatched adventure for all visitors. Thanks to the efforts of visionaries, including Jay Sarno, Kirk Kerkorian, the management of Circus Circus, and Steve Wynn, Las Vegas visitors can now start at one end of the Strip and, over a period of several days, work their way down the Fabulous Boulevard, partaking of a cornucopia of attractions unlike those found anywhere else in the world.

In fewer than ninety years, Las Vegas has grown from a rough desert village to the world's premier tourist spot. The bright lights, huge hotels, and many fantasy attractions justify beyond imagination the hopes of the town's early boosters, such as Pop Squires, Maxwell Kelch, and even Howard Hughes.

In the 1930s businessmen in a dusty little railroad town located on the ragged edge of civilization found that legalized gambling attracted visitors. They soon discovered that business improved when gamers were provided rooms, food, and entertainment. During the 1950s and 1960s hotels got larger and more luxurious; big, elaborate production shows became popular; the rich and famous began frequenting the casinos and showrooms; and people from all walks of life flocked to Las Vegas. Soon the name Las Vegas became synonymous with gaming and star-powered entertainment. By the late 1980s resort operators discovered that megasized resorts built around a theme meant megasized profits. This realization ushered in a new era in Las Vegas history. Those with the economic resources to construct and properly operate huge gaming palaces prosper; those that don't are either absorbed by large operators or fall by the wayside. In the meantime, burgeoning growth in the Las Vegas Valley is producing a deteriorating quality of life for the city's residents, including increased air pollution, traffic congestion, a shortage of public parks, higher taxes, and crowded schools. No one knows where such exponential growth w+-ill eventually lead.

Some sages predict that the spread of legalized gambling to other communities in this country and overseas will have a negative effect on Las Vegas or that the public's interest in gambling will fade and shrink the pool of potential visitors. Given its spectacular history, it would be foolish to assume that the curtain will fall on Las Vegas as the center stage for world entertainment. The growing interest in gambling and the rising number of people who travel for business and pleasure will undoubtedly result in an increase in the number of people who visit Las Vegas. One can but wonder what entertainment extravaganzas will greet future visitors to Las Vegas, The Great American Playground.

References

"A View from the Top." *Nevada Casino Journal*. May 1991.

Demaris, Ovid. "You and I Are Very Different from Howard Hughes." *Esquire*. March 1969.

Green, Marian. "Wynn Details Bellagio's Grand Plan." *Las Vegas Review-Journal*. March 7, 1996.

———. "Vanishing into the Sands of Time." *Las Vegas Review-Journal*. June 30, 1996.

Hess, Alan. "A Lost Place in the Sun." *Las Vegas Review-Journal*. July 14, 1996.

Kaufman, Perry. "The Best City of Them All: A History of Las Vegas, 1930–1960." Ph.D. dissertation. University of California at Santa Barbara. 1974.

Kelly, Isabel T., and Catherine S. Fowler. "Southern Paiute." *Handbook of North American Indians: Great Basin*, Warren L. D'Azevedo, ed., vol. 11, pp. 368–397. Washington, D.C.: Smithsonian Institute. 1986.

Lewis, Georgia. *North Las Vegas History*. North Las Vegas: Chamber of Commerce. 1976.

Lingenfelter, Richard E. *Death Valley and the Amargosa: A Land of Illusion*. Berkeley, CA: University of California Press. 1986.

Moehring, Eugene P. *Resort City in the Sunbelt: Las Vegas, 1930–1970*. Las Vegas: University of Nevada. 1989.

Palermo, Dave. "Aiming for Popular Elegance." *Las Vegas Review-Journal*. June 16, 1996.

———. "Quiet Man Behind MGM Grand Not Expected at Grand Opening." *Las Vegas Review-Journal/Sun*. December 12, 1993.

Squires, Charles P., and Delphine A. Squires. "Las Vegas, Nevada: Its Romance and History." Unpublished manuscript. Special Collections, University of Nevada, Las Vegas. 1955.

Stamos, George, Jr. "El Rancho Vegas—The Great Resorts of Las Vegas: How They Began, Part 1." *Las Vegas Sun Magazine*. Pp. 6–11. April 1, 1979a.

————. "Flamingo Hotel—The Great Resorts of Las Vegas: How They Began, Part 3." *Las Vegas Sun Magazine*. Pp. 6–11. April 22, 1979b.

————. "Sands Hotel—The Great Resorts of Las Vegas: How They Began, Part 7." *Las Vegas Sun Magazine*. Pp. 6–11. June 17, 1979c.

————. "Dunes Hotel and Country Club—The Great Resorts of Las Vegas: How They Began, Part 9." *Las Vegas Sun Magazine*. Pp. 6–11. July 15, 1979d.

Stewart, Helen J. Letter to George S. Sawyer, attorney in Pioche, Nevada. Helen J. Stewart Collection, Nevada State Museum and Historical Society, Las Vegas, Nevada. July 16, 1884.

Townley, Carrie Miller. "Helen J. Stewart: First Lady of Las Vegas." *Nevada Historical Society Quarterly*, vol. 16, no. 4, pp. 215–244. 1973.

Suggested Readings

Jones, Florence Lee, and John F. Cahlan. *Water: A History of Las Vegas*. 2 Volumes. Las Vegas: Las Vegas Valley Water District. 1975.

Kaufman, Perry. "The Best City of Them All: A History of Las Vegas, 1930–1960." Ph.D. dissertation. University of California at Santa Barbara. 1974.

Kelly, Isabel T., and Catherine S. Fowler. "Southern Paiute." *Handbook of North American Indians: Great Basin*, Warren L. D'Azevedo, ed., vol. 11, pp. 368–397. Washington, D.C.: Smithsonian Institute. 1986.

Knepp, Donn. *Las Vegas: The Entertainment Capital*. Menlo Park, CA: Lane Publishing Co. 1987.

Moehring, Eugene P. *Resort City in the Sunbelt: Las Vegas, 1930–1970*. Las Vegas: University of Nevada. 1989.

Paher, Stanley W. *Las Vegas: As it Began, As It Grew*. Las Vegas: Nevada Publications. 1971.

Puzo, Mario. *Inside Las Vegas*. New York: Grosset & Dunlop. 1977.

Roske, Ralph J. *Las Vegas: A Desert Paradise*. Tulsa, OK: Continental Herigate Press. 1986.

Squires, Charles P., and Delphine A. Squires. "Las Vegas, Nevada: Its Romance and History." Unpublished manuscript. Special Collections, University of Nevada, Las Vegas. 1955.

Stamos, George, Jr. A series of articles on the history of Las Vegas casinos. "The Great Resorts of Las Vegas: How They Began." *Las Vegas Sun Magazine*. April through December 1979.

MAP SHOWING LOCATIONS OF MOST MAJOR RESORTS OF LAS VEGAS

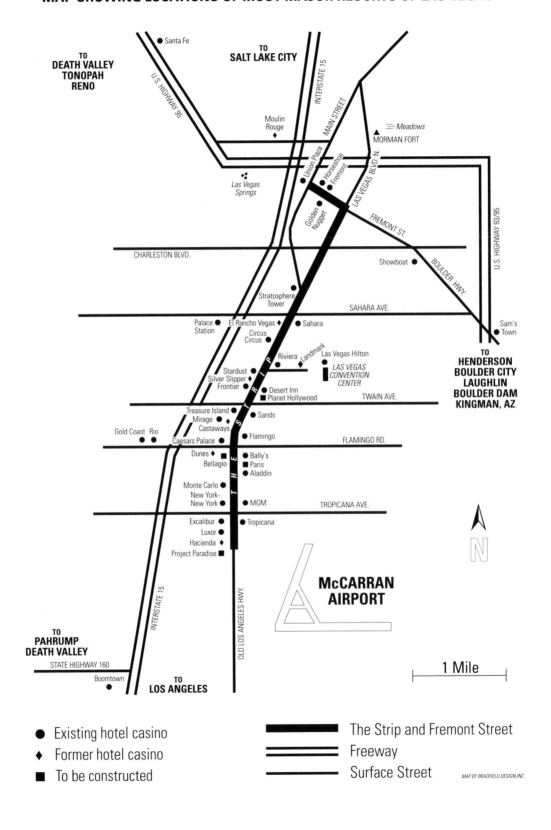

● Santa Fe

TO DEATH VALLEY TONOPAH RENO

TO SALT LAKE CITY

INTERSTATE 15

MAIN STREET

U.S. HIGHWAY 95

Moulin Rouge ◆

≡ Meadows
▲ MORMAN FORT

Union Plaza ●
Horseshoe
Fremont

Las Vegas Springs

LAS VEGAS BLVD. N.

Golden Nugget ◆

FREMONT ST.

CHARLESTON BLVD.

Showboat ●

BOULDER HWY.

U.S. HIGHWAY 93/95

Stratosphere Tower ●

SAHARA AVE.

Palace Station ●
El Rancho Vegas ◆ ● Sahara
Circus Circus ●

Sam's Town ●

Riviera ● Landmark ◆ Las Vegas Hilton ●

Stardust ●
Silver Slipper ◆
Frontier ●

LAS VEGAS CONVENTION CENTER

TO HENDERSON BOULDER CITY LAUGHLIN BOULDER DAM KINGMAN, AZ

Desert Inn ●
Planet Hollywood ■

TWAIN AVE.

Treasure Island ●
Mirage ● ● Sands
Castaways ◆

Gold Coast Rio
● ●
Caesars Palace ● ● Flamingo

FLAMINGO RD.

THE STRIP

Dunes ◆
Bellagio ●
● Bally's
■ Paris
● Aladdin

Monte Carlo ●
New York-New York ●
● MGM

TROPICANA AVE.

Excalibur ●
Luxor ●
Hacienda ●
Project Paradise ■

● Tropicana

McCARRAN AIRPORT

N

INTERSTATE 15

OLD LOS ANGELES HWY.

TO PAHRUMP DEATH VALLEY

STATE HIGHWAY 160

Boomtown ●

TO LOS ANGELES

1 Mile

● Existing hotel casino
◆ Former hotel casino
■ To be constructed

▬▬▬ The Strip and Fremont Street
═══ Freeway
──── Surface Street

MAP BY BRADFIELD DESIGN, INC.

Continuation of Chapter 1 Illustration Caption

The horse and burro's bones (members of the genus Equus*) would have been largely indistinguishable from those of the modern Arabian horse and the burros running wild on the desert today. In the distance are 7-foot-tall camels (*Camelops hesternus*); an American lion (*Panthera leo*), very similar to the modern African lion, can be seen protesting the presence of two Columbian mammoths (*Mammuthus columbi*), who stood twelve feet tall and weighed about 10,000 pounds. A Shasta ground sloth (*Nothrotheriops shastenis*), weighing about 1,000 pounds, is dining on a Joshua tree. In the foreground at right is a coyote; at left, a giant short-faced bear (*Arctodus simus*), who was 30 percent larger than the present-day grizzly, can be seen looking the situation over. In the sky, an Incredible teratorn (*Teratornis incredibilis*), a relative of the vulture—and, with its 16- to 17-foot wing span one of the largest flying birds ever—soars on a thermal updraft. Juniper trees and sagebrush were common on the valley floor. All animals pictured here except the human and the coyote became extinct in the New World by about 10,000 years ago. Looking southwest across the valley is Mount Potosi, where the life of the great film star Carole Lombard ended in a plane crash 11,000 years later.* Drawing by Gary Raham, Wellington, Colorado, with consulting by W. Geoffrey Spaulding

About the Author

Robert D. McCracken received a Ph.D. in cultural anthropology from the University of Colorado. He has taught at several colleges and universities, including Colorado Women's College, California State University at Long Beach, and UCLA. He has conducted research with a variety of groups and communities, primarily in the western United States. He has written more than a dozen books on the history of Nevada, and this volume is the result of ten years of study on the history and culture of Las Vegas.

Index

[*italic* entries indicate photos]

African Americans, 14, 46, *47, 129*
Agriculture, 14, 15, 28
Aladdin Hotel and Casino, 115
Ali, Muhammad, *91*
Anasazi, 3
Anderson Camp, 46
Apache Club, 41, 42
Arden, Donn, 95
Arizona Club, 24, *24, 25,* 56
Armijo, Antonio, 7
Ash Meadows, 3
Aviation, 30, *31*

Bacall, Lauren, *74*
Bacharach, Burt, 95
Ball, Lucille, 95
Bally Entertainment Corporation, 113
Bally's, *60,* 87, 95, *96,* 113
Barbary Coast, *60, 89*
Basic Magnesium Processing Plant, 46, *47*
Bayley, Judy, 130
Bayley, Warren "Doc," 130
Beatles, 72
Bell, Lieutenant Governor Rex, 78
Bellagio, 112, *112*
Bennett, William G., 92, 100, 109, 115
Bergen, Edgar, 70
Berle, Milton, 54
Berman, Lyle, 106
Big Springs, 14
Bingo Palace, 117, *117*
Binion, Benny, 97, *97*
Bishop, Joey, 73, 125

Black Canyon, *34,* 35
Block 16, 23–25, *23, 24, 25,* 37, 39
Blue Diamond, 117
Boomtown Hotel-Casino, 117
Boulder Canyon, 33, 35
Boulder City, *36, 37,* 37–38, 46, 50, 51
Boulder Club, 42
Boulder Dam. *See* Hoover Dam
Boulder Station, 117
Bowlon, Fletcher, 69
Boyd, Bill, 97
Boyd, Sam, 97, *97*
Bringhurst, William, 9, *10*
Buol, Peter, 28
Burton, Lance, 108
Bush, President George, 48

Caesars Palace, 60, 64, *89, 90,* 90–92, *91, 92, 114,* 115
Cahlan, John, 50
Caliente, Nevada, 30
California Hotel, 97, 110
Caravan Room Restaurant, 71
Carnival Lounge, 77
Caroll, Frank, 128
Carson, Kit, 8
Carver Park, 46
Carville, Edward P. "Ted," 53
Casbah Lounge, 71
Casino, 118
Casino de Paris, 122
Castaways, 89, 121, *129*
Chaney, Lon, 118

Charleston Mountains, 16
Charleston Peak, 1, 3
Cherry 2000, 118, *119*
Chief Tecopa, 4, *4*
Circus Circus, 91–92, *93,* 101, 107–108, 113, 131
Circus Circus Enterprises, 100, 101, 109, 113, 115, 130
Cirque du Soleil, 112, 116
Clark, Wilbur, 69–70, *70*
Clark, Senator William A., 18–19, 21, 22, 30
Clark County, 7, 41, 42, 46, 53
Clark land auction, *20,* 22–23, *26,* 27
Clark townsite, *20,* 22, 28, 39
Cloud Nine Lounge, 56, *61*
Clover Room, 76
Clovis culture, 2
Club Bingo. *See* Sahara
Cobb, Lee J., 118
Cole, Nat King, 54
Colorado River, 1, 3, 7, 13, *32,* 33–35, 37
Colorado River Power Company, 33
Congo Room, 71
Copa, 73
Coppola, Francis Ford, 118
Cornero, Tony, 41, *43, 80,* 81
Costello, Frank, 79
Costello, Lou, 122
Cottonwood Island, 3
Crawford, Michael, *116*
Crosby, Bing, 72

Darin, Bobby, 95
Davis, Sammy, Jr., 54, *61, 73*
Day, Doris, *74*
Death Valley, 8, 13
Dellenbaugh, Frederick S., *11*
Del Webb Corporation, 64
Desert Inn, 69–70, *70,* 75, 81, 88, 89, 115
Desert Palace. *See* Caesars Palace
Desert Villa Motel, *89*
Diller, Phyllis, 95
Divorce, ix, 39–40, *40*
Double-O, 24
Dude ranches, 40
Dunes Hotel, *60,* 64, *84, 98,* 112, *112, 120,* 121–23, *122*
Durante, Jimmy, 54, 63

Eckstine, Billy, 73
EFX, 116
El Cortez Hotel, 60, 79, 110
El Dorado Canyon, 13, 14, 15
Eldorado Club, 97
Electric Horseman, The, 118

El Rancho, 64, 84
El Rancho Vegas, *48,* 51, *52,* 53–54, *54, 55,* 56, *66,* 69, 75, 115, 121, 124
Ely, Sims, 38
Entratter, Jack, 73
Evans, Dale, 118
Excalibur Hotel and Casino, *78,* 100–101, *110,* 113, 115

Factor, John, 81
Factor, Rella, 81
Fertitta, Frank, Jr., 117
Fisher, Eddie, 78
Fitzgerald's, 110
Flamingo Capri Motel, *89*
Flamingo Hotel, 60–63, *60, 61, 62, 66, 67,* 75, 76, *84, 89, 90,* 94, 95, 117
Folies Bergères, *79*
Four Queens, 110
Four Seasons Hotel, 113
Fremont, Colonel John Charles, 8, *8*
Fremont Hotel, 77, 97, 110
Fremont Street, 23, *27, 28, 30, 31,* 39, 41, 64, *65*
Fremont Street Experience, 110, *111*
Friedman, Jake, 72
Frontier, 89
Fuller, Zelpha Daedura, 10

Gabbs, Nevada, 46
Gable, Clark, *40, 50,* 50–51
Gable, Ria Langham, 40
Gambling: legislation of, in Nevada, ix, 38, 39, 40–43; and growth of Las Vegas, 41, 53, 131–32
Gaming Control Board, 87
Garces, Father Francisco, 7
Garland, Judy, 41, *123*
Gass, Octavius Decatur, *11,* 13–14, 15, 17
Gaughan, Jackie, 117
Gaughan, Michael, 117
Gem, 24
Gleason, Jackie, 54
Glitter Gulch. *See* Fremont Street
Godey, Alex, 8
Gold Coast, 117
Golden Camel, 41
Golden Gate, 110
Golden Hotel, *30*
Golden Nugget, 64, *64, 65,* 102, 110
Goldfield, Nevada, 22
Gold Strike Resorts, 107
Goodsprings, 7
Gottlieb, Jake, 122
Grand Casinos, Inc., 106

Grand Slam Canyon, 101
Grant, Cary, *74*, 95
Great Depression, *36*, 37
Greenbaum, Gus, *62*, 63, 76
Griffith, R. E., *56*
Gumm, Frances. *See* Judy Garland
Gumm Sisters, 41
Gypsum culture, 3

Hacienda Hotel, *59*, 113, 130, *130*
Hal Roach Studios, 118
Ham, Art, Sr., 64
Hard Rock Hotel, 117
Harrah's, 115
Harriman, Edward H., 18
Hazards of Helen, 118
Helldorado, 118
Henderson, Charles, 46
Henderson, Nevada, 46, *47*
Henry, Schyler, 16–17
Hess, Alan, 124
Hill, Virginia, 63
Hilton Hotel, 87, *116*
Holiday Inn, 87
Holmes, Larry, *91*
Honeymoon in Las Vegas, 118
Hoover Dam, ix, *32*, 33–38, *34*, *35*, 45, 46, 75
Horseshoe Club, 97, 110
Hotel Las Vegas, *26*, 27
Houssels, J. Kell, 79
Howell, John, 14
Hughes, Howard, 87–89, *88*, 111, 128, *129*, 131
Hull, Thomas, 53–54, 56
Humperdinck, Englebert, 95
Hyatt Hotel, 87

Imperial Palace, *89*
Indian Springs, 2, 3
International Hotel, *94*, 95

J. Walter Thompson Company, 66
Jackie Gaughan's Plaza, 110
Jaffe, Ben, 78, 79
Jean, Nevada, 7
Jessel, George, 63
Jo Ann Jordan Trio, 77

Kastel, Phil, 79
Kaye, Danny, 72
Kefauver, Senator Estes, 87
Kelch, Maxwell, 65, *65*, 69, 131
Kelly, Grace, *74*
Kerkorian, Kirk, *94*, 94–95, 104, 109, 131
Kiel, Conrad, 15, 16, 17

Kiel, Edwin, 16, *17*, 18
Kiel, William, *17*, 18
Kiel Ranch, 15–18, *16*, 19, 21, 28, *29*, *40*
Knapp, Albert, 10
Korean War, 46
Kyle Ranch. *See* Kiel Ranch

Ladd, Captain James H., 27
Ladd's Hotel, 27
Lake Mojave culture, 2–3
Landmark, 89, *89*, 121, 128, *128*
Lansky, Meyer, 60
LaRue Restaurant, 72
Last Frontier, *25*, 56, *56–59*, *61*, *66*, *67*, 69, 75, *84*, 88, 89
Las Vegas: founding of, 18, 21, 22–23; population of, ix, x, 30, 45, 99, 132; visitors to, x, 99
Las Vegas Club, 110
Las Vegas Colony, 9
Las Vegas Convention Center, *83*, 83–84, *89*
Las Vegas Fort, 9, 13–14, *15*
Las Vegas Hilton, *94*, 118
Las Vegas Hotel, *26*
Las Vegas Mission, 10
Las Vegas Ranch, 14, 15, 19
Las Vegas Springs, 1, 9, 19
Las Vegas Story, The, 118, 119
Las Vegas Valley, ix, 1, 2, 3, 7, 9, 10, *11*, 13, 15, 16, 18, 19, 21, 28
Las Vegas Wash, 7
Lawford, Peter, 73
Laxalt, Paul, 88
Leaving Las Vegas, 118
Lee, Peggy, 54
Levinson, Ed, 77
Lewis, Jerry, 54, *74*
Lewis, Joe E., 62
Liberace, *85*
Lido de Paris, *80*, *81*, 82, *82*
Limited Test Ban Treaty, 48
Liston, Sonny, 115
Little Church of the West, 56, *57*, *59*
Lombard, Carole, 40, *50*, 50–51
Longstreet, Jack, 16
Los Angeles Terminal Railroad, 18
Lost in America, 118
Louis, Joe, *91*
Luciano, Lucky, 60
Luxor, 101, *101*, 113

Mailer, Norman, *123*
Main Street Station, 110
Manilow, Barry, 95
Marina Hotel, 104

Martin, Dean, 54, 73, *74*, 95
Mary Kay Trio, 61
Masterplan Mile, 113
Mature, Victor, 118
McAfee, Captain Guy, 40, 53, *56*, 64
McAllister, Wayne, 124
McCarran International Airport, x, 45
McCracken, Bambi, *119*
McIntosh, J. C. "Jim," 24
McWilliams, J. T., 21, 22
McWilliams townsite, 21–22
Meadows Club, 41, *43*, 81
Meadows Mall, 8
Meadow Valley Wash, 18, 28
MGM Grand, 78, 87, 95, *96*, *104*, 104–105, 116
Mining: and development of Las Vegas, 10, *11*, 13, 14, 22, 45, 46
Minsky's Follies, 122
Mint Hotel, 97
Mirage, 102–03, *102*, *103*, 116, 121, 125, 129
Mirage Resorts, Inc., 107, 112, 123
Mojave Desert, 1, 3, 7
Monte Carlo Club, 69
Monte Carlo Resort and Casino, 107–08, *108*, 112
Moore, William J. (Bill), 56, *59*, 75
Mormons, 9, 10, 11, 13, 15
Mormon Fort, *15*
Mormon Trail (Road), 8, 9, 14, 18
Moulin Rouge, *129*
Mount Potosi, 10, *11*, 50
Muggs, J. Fred, *79*

Nellis Air Force Base, 30, 45–46, 50
Nevada Test Site, 48–49, 77
New Frontier, 56, *61*
Newhart, Bob, 124
Newman, Paul, *55*
Newton, Jerry, 77
Newton, Wayne, 77
New York–Chicago–San Francisco trade route, 18
New York–New York, 109–110, *109*
91-Club, 40, 56
Northern Club, *31*, 41, *42*
North Las Vegas, 28–29, *29*, 37

Ocean's 11, 118
One From the Heart, 118
One Million B.C., 118
Oregon Building, *60*, *62*
Oregon Short Line, 18
Overton, Nevada, 2

Pahrump, Nevada, 2
Pahrump Valley, 7, 8
Pair-O-Dice Club, 41, 53, 56, *56*, 121
Palace Station. *See* Bingo Palace
Palance, Jack, 118
Paradise Road, 94, 95
Paris Casino and Resort, 113, *113*
Parish, Hank, 16, 17
Patterson, Floyd, *123*
Pennington, William N., 92
Perlman, Clifford, 91
Peters, Jean, *88*, 89, 128
Pinto Basin culture, 3
Planet Hollywood, 115
Players Club, *69*
Potosi Mine, *11*, 13
Powell, Jane, 73
Prell, Milton, 71
Presley, Elvis, 72, *85*, 95, 118, *119*
Presley, Priscilla Beaulieu, *119*
Primadonna Resorts, 109
Primm, Gary E., 109
Prohibition, 29, 39
Prostitution, 25, 37, 39
Puzo, Mario, 67

Radio stations, 65
Raft, George, 95
Railroad: and development of Las Vegas, 18–19, 28, 30, 45
Rainman, 118
Rawls, Lou, 77
Reagan, Ronald, *58*
Redford, Robert, 118
Red Onion, 24
Reno, Nevada, 2, 22
Rex, King of the Wild Horses, 118
Rex, S.S., *80*, 81
Riddle, Major Arteburn, 64, 122
Riklis, Meshulam, 76
Rio, 117
Rivera, Rafael, 7
Rivers, Joan, 95
Riviera Hotel, 76, *76*, *83*, *84*, 121
Roach, Hal, 118
Rockwell, Leon, 31
Rockwell Field, 30, *31*
Rogers, Roy, 118
Roosevelt, Eleanor, *34*
Roosevelt, President Franklin Delano, *34*, 35
Rosen, Morris, 62, 63
Royal Nevada, 121
Russell, Jane, 118, *119*
Ryolite, Nevada, 22, 24

Sahara Hotel, *71*, 71–72, *86*, *89*, 97
Salt Lake City, Utah, 8, 9, 18
Samís Town, 97, 117
Sands Hotel, *66*, *68*, 72–73, *72*, *73*, *74*, *86*, 88, 89, 113, *114*, 124–27, *124*, *125*, *127*
San Pedro, Los Angeles, and Salt Lake Railroad, 18, *19*, 22, 30
Sans Souci, *129*
Santa Fe Casino, 117
Sarno, Jay, 90, 91, 92, 131
Schmidt, Henry C., 33
Scorsese, Martin, 118
Scott, Frank, 97
Sedway, Moe, *62*, 63
Showboat, 75, *75*, 79, 117
Siegel, Ben "Bugsy," 60–63, *61*, 89
Siegfried and Roy, *102*, 103, 116
Silverbird, 64
Silver Slipper, 89, *129*
Sinatra, Frank, 73, *74*, 125
Sinatra, Nancy, 95
Southern Paiute, 3–4, *5*, 9
Spanish Trail, 7, 8
Spring Mountains, 4
Squires, C. P. "Pop," 27, 131
Stardust, *80*, 81–82, *82*, 97, 105
Starlight Express, 116
Starlight Lounge, 82
Starr, Kay, 77
Star Ship Orion, 115
Stern, Martin, Jr., 124
Stewart, Archibald, 11, 14, 15, 16, 17, 18
Stewart, Frank, 17
Stewart, Helen, 9, *14*, 15, 16, 17, 19, 21
Stewart, Will, 17
Stewart Ranch, *11*, *12*, 15, *15*, 17, 19, 21
Stralla, Anthony. *See* Cornero, Tony
Stratosphere Tower, 105–107, *106*, *107*
Streisand, Barbra, 95, 105
Strip, The, 53, *54*, 56, 59, 60, 63, *65*, *66*, 69, 71, 75, 76, 77, 78, 81, *84*, *86*, 89, *89*, 95, *96*, 99, 104, 105, 106, *107*, 109, 113, *119*
Stupak, Bob, 105–06, 126
Sultan's Table, 122

Temperance, 23
They Came to Rob Las Vegas, 118
Thomas, Danny, 73
Thomas, E. Parry, 102
Thomas, Roscoe, 64
Thunderbird, 63–64, *67*, 84
Tonopah, Nevada, 22, 89
Torres, Ed, 64
Tracy, Spencer, 51

Treasure Island, 103, *103*
Tropicana Hotel, 78–79, *78*, *79*, *85*, 89, 104
Tule Springs, 2

Union Pacific Railroad, 18, 19, 30
Union Plaza Hotel, 97, 117
Union Railroad Station, *27*, 97

Valley of Fire, *118*
Vegas Club, 42
Vegas Vacation, 118
Vegas Verde. *See* North Las Vegas
Vegas World Hotel, 105
Victory Village, 46
Viva Las Vegas, 118
Volstead Act, 29

Walker, Joseph, 8
Walters, Lou, 79
Wee Kirk of the Heather Wedding Chapel, *39*
Weismuller, Johnny, *91*
Welch, Raquel, 95
Western Air Express, 30, 45
Western Airlines. *See* Western Air Express
Wiley, Roland, 53
Wilkerson, William, Sr., 60
Williams, Andy, 54, 91
Williams, Tom, 28, 29
Williams, Wayne C., 50, 51
Wilson, James B., 14
Wood, Natalie, 95
Woodward, Joanne, *55*
World War I, 33
World War II, ix, 45, 46, 50, 81, 97
Wynn, Steve, 102, *102*, 103, 107, 109, 112, 123, 131

Young, Brigham, 9